Philip Derriman is a journalist in Sydney, Australia, who writes frequently on cricket. He is the author of three other books.

PHILIP DERRIMAN

Bodyline

GRAFTON BOOKS

A Division of the Collins Publishing Group

LONDON GLASGOW
TORONTO SYDNEY AUCKLAND

Grafton Books
A Division of the Collins Publishing Group
8 Grafton Street, London W1X 3LA

Published by Grafton Books 1986

First published in Australia by
Fontana Books 1984

Copyright © Kennedy Miller Pty Ltd 1984

ISBN 0-586-06676-4

Printed and bound in Great Britain by
Collins, Glasgow

Set in Times

Contents

Introduction 7
1 The Target 9
2 Jardine 17
3 Captain of England 29
4 A Plan is Born 36
5 The Trap is Sprung 51
6 McCabe's Finest Hour 66
7 Bradman's Triumph 75
8 Shocks at Adelaide 87
9 Controversy to Crisis 102
10 Rebuff from Lord's 116
11 A Secret Intervention 121
12 A Kind of Peace 132
13 The Last Act 142
14 A Reassessment 151
15 Repercussions 159
16 Loose Ends 167
Biographies 172
Appendices
  A: Scoring rates 197
  B: Test Scores 198

Introduction

'I do not think there was one single batsman who played in most of those bodyline games who ever afterwards recaptured his love for cricket.'

Jack Fingleton

Bodyline was probably not, as some have suggested, an inevitable development in cricket. On the contrary – it was, in a sense, highly improbable, for there could not have been bodyline if there had not been a rare conjunction of circumstances and people, three of whom, in particular, were essential to it. First, a batsman whose mastery over bowlers was such that special, desperate measures had to be devised to combat him. Second, a captain daring enough to conceive the bodyline strategy, ruthless enough to implement it, and, more important still, courageous enough to persevere with it in the face of a nation's rage. Third, a bowler of exceptional pace, accuracy and hostility to put the strategy into effect. Finally, the drama required that these characters meet on the same stage, at the same moment of history, when each was at the height of his powers. This is what happened in Australia in 1932–33.

1
The Target

Don Bradman was only twenty-four years old when Douglas Jardine, cricket captain of England, set out to overcome him with the kind of bowling which came to be called bodyline. This is worth keeping in mind, for it helps to provide a better understanding of the real nature of the bodyline phenomenon. England's cricketers did not turn to bodyline as a last resort, after trying and failing to counter Bradman with other means. Rather, they turned to it in haste and panic, after Bradman, at the age of twenty-two, had had one spectacularly successful season against them, in England in 1930. Jardine was seeking to knock Bradman off his pedestal, but it was a pedestal Bradman had only just begun to occupy.

Bradman came up from his home town, Bowral, to play first-grade cricket in Sydney in 1926–27, when he was eighteen. He got into the NSW side in 1927–8, when he was nineteen, and got into the Australian side in 1928–29, when he was twenty. It was a startlingly rapid advancement, but Bradman took it all in his stride. His confidence in his own ability was such that he was never overawed by an occasion. In England in 1930, Bradman achieved a degree of mastery over bowlers which no batsman had approached before him and none has approached since. He was dismissed thirty-two times during the tour and made four centuries, five double centuries and one triple century. The better the bowling, the better he seemed to perform. Against the cream of England's bowlers in the Tests,

Harold Larwood and Maurice Tate among them, he
made the following scores: 8, 131, 254, 1, 334, 14, 232.
Thus, in five Tests he had scored 974 runs at an average
of 139.

It does not seem there was anyone who played with
or against Bradman who did not regard his ability as
freakish. His talents were such that it seemed nature
had fashioned him specifically for the task of scoring
runs. Bill O'Reilly, who saw more of Bradman over a
longer period than anyone, expressed this very thought.
'Bradman was absolutely unique,' O'Reilly said. 'He
had a brain that was built by God as a one-offer. It
was custom built for the job of playing cricket.' Bradman was a short man, whose height has been estimated
variously between 5′ 6¾″ (169.5 cm) and 5′ 8″ (172.7
cm). He was slim but by no means slight, and after his
triumphs in England in 1930 Pelham Warner listed
physical strength as one of the keys to his success.
'Short in height, though long in the leg, and with very
broad shoulders,' Warner wrote, 'he is, from a cricket
point of view, finely and compactly built, and one was
particularly struck by the fit of his cricket boots on his
small feet.' Those small feet were the foundation of
Bradman's batsmanship. Footwork was the essence of
his game, and in his younger days it was common for
commentators to liken the speed and lightness of his
feet to those of a ballet dancer.

Yet of the millions of words written about Bradman,
it is remarkable how few of them sought to describe
his batting style. An English writer once complained
that Bradman's strokes seemed to be over in a twink-
ling, too fast for the eye to record them in the memory,
but it is more likely that writers found it difficult to
describe Bradman's batting style because it was not
idiosyncratic. It was not made distinctive, as the styles

of many other batsmen are, by various mannerisms or affectations.

Anyone too young to have seen Bradman bat will discover the kind of batsman he was only by watching newsreel films of him. Certain features of his batting will then become apparent. For instance, he kept completely still while awaiting the ball. His bat did not tap and his feet did not shuffle. He had a pronounced follow-through, and it is common to see him on film complete a vigorous stroke such as a drive with his bat resting against his spine, rather like a golfer. If it were necessary to categorize Bradman's batting on the evidence of the newsreel films, it might be said that he was a hitter rather than a stroker of the ball. This does not mean, of course, that his shots in any way lacked refinement. It means simply that to see Bradman play an attacking shot is to see a very positive, decisive, vigorous, even violent movement, not one of effortless grace.

In the 1930 Tests Bradman scored at the rate of 3.7 runs for every six balls faced, which would be reckoned a brisk rate today even in a one-day match. Some English bowlers suffered more than others. Off Harold Larwood, Bradman scored at the astonishing rate of 5.6 runs for each six balls faced. Larwood took such a hammering from Bradman that he was dropped for one Test. 'He murdered me,' Larwood later admitted. Off Gubby Allen, who may have bowled even faster than Larwood in 1930, Bradman scored at the rate of 6.0 runs for each six balls faced. What most impressed English commentators who watched Bradman in 1930 was not just that he scored as many runs as he did, as fast as he did, but that he scored them with a minimum of risk. This provided the theme for Neville Cardus'

well-known treatise on Bradman in 1930. Cardus
wrote:

> 'It was as though the sheer finish of technique was a prison
> for his spirit. He could not make a hazardous flight; he
> reminded me of the trapeze performer who one night decided
> to commit suicide by flinging himself headlong to the stage,
> but could not achieve the error because his skill had become
> infallible, a routined and mechanical habit not at the beck
> and call of anything so volatile as human will or impulse.
> When Bradman passed 200 at Leeds I felt that my interest in
> his play might break out anew at the sight of one miscalculated
> stroke. But none was to be seen.'

It is interesting that English observers should have
found Bradman's batting so secure, so free of weak-
nesses, in 1930, for they did not all find it so in
1928–29. One English critic in particular, Percy Fender,
who covered the 1928–29 tour for an English newspaper, wrote disparagingly about Bradman's technique. Even when Fender praised him, his praise
invariably was qualified. The theme of his comments
was that Bradman was brilliant but unsound. Fender
pursued this theme in a book he wrote afterwards
about the 1928–29 series, *The Turn of the Wheel*.
'Bradman was one of the most curious mixtures of
good and bad batting I have ever seen,' Fender wrote.
'. . . One would see him cram half a dozen or more
shots, worthy of the greatest, into a couple or three
overs, then two or three times running he would
completely mis-time, mis-judge, and mis-hit the ball.
One minute one would think him a grand player, and
the next he would look like a schoolboy.' Fender never
met Bradman, so his criticism was entirely impersonal.
It does not seem, however, that Bradman received the
criticism impersonally. That he took exception to it is

evident from the fact that he referred to it in two books he wrote about himself, *Don Bradman's Book* in 1931 and *Farewell to Cricket* in 1949.

Fender was one of the game's personalities. He was 6′ 2″ (188 cm) tall, and his moustache, his spectacles and his dark, crinkly hair reminded people of Groucho Marx. Born in August 1892, he played county cricket immediately before the First World War and played for England in the first two Test series against Australia after the war. His Test career was brief and undistinguished, and it was as captain of Surrey in the 1920s that he established his reputation. Arthur Carr, who in Fender's day was captain of Nottinghamshire and, briefly, captain of England, wrote that Fender was the best English captain never to captain England. One reason he was not given the England captaincy, probably, was that he was outspoken and nonconformist by nature and had several brushes with the MCC's officialdom.

Fender has only a supporting role in the bodyline story, but it is an important role nevertheless, for he provides a most interesting link between Jardine and Bradman. Fender and Jardine had played together for Surrey for a number of years and had become good friends, and Jardine had deep admiration for Fender as a captain and tactician. Towards the end of May 1930, the Australians came to the Oval to play Surrey. Fender and Jardine were in the Surrey side and Bradman in the Australian. Even at this early stage of the tour, Bradman was the talk of the Australian team. After six matches he had a batting average of 111.66, and most of his runs had been scored at a fantastically fast rate. It may be that by then Fender had come to revise his earlier opinion of Bradman's batting. He would have heard of Bradman's prodigious scoring in the 1929–30 season in Australia, when he made the world record score of 452 not out, and like most other Englishmen he must have been impressed by Bradman's successes on the tour so far. Now he had to oppose Bradman on the field himself, and if he thought at all of his criticism of the Australian in the previous year it may well have been with regret.

In the book he wrote the following year, *Don Bradman's Book*, Bradman said:

> 'I hope for pardon when I say I had a particularly personal reason for looking forward to my first match against Surrey. Mr Fender, the Surrey captain, besides being a great captain of a great county, is also a leading critic of his country; and if I have not misunderstood him, he did not think too highly of my batting or my fielding during the last series of Tests in Australia. I am not at all susceptible to criticism, but I need not make any secret of the fact that I was filled with a quiet determination to do well at the Oval.'

The tone of this makes it clear that Bradman had a score to settle with Fender on the field. It was when he was in this frame of mind, bowlers everywhere were to discover, that Bradman was most dangerous.

Australia batted first, and the early dismissal of one of the openers brought Bradman to the crease at 12.45 P.M. It was an overcast day, and Bradman batted without a cap, as he often did early in his career. He began cautiously, no doubt in deference to the importance of the occasion, and took 90 minutes to get to 50. Then, as if he had satisfied himself that he had nothing to fear from the pitch or the bowling, he set upon the Surrey attack with a ferocity which was exceptional even for him. He went from 50 to 100 in less than an hour and from 100 to 200 in only 80 minutes. At the end of the day he was unbeaten on

252, his only error having been a chance to short leg when he was 207. Edward Docker gave the following description of Bradman's innings in his book, *Bradman and the Bodyline Series*:

> 'He began to unleash that terrible weapon of destruction, the pull shot. Fender was bowling with a packed off-side field and only a deep mid-on on the other side of the wicket. But Bradman would get right outside his off stump and pivoting on his right foot smash the ball forward of square-leg. Twice he played this same shot. Fender pulled a man out of the covers to block it. Bradman stroked the third ball back along the pitch, leapt at the next and drove it through the vacant spot in the covers. The cross-bat may have offended against all the canons of classical batsmanship, but Fender was perhaps too occupied with field settings and bowling changes to spare the matter a critical thought.'

Docker says that when Bradman returned to the dressing room he threw down his gloves and said, 'I wonder what Fender will have to say in the morning papers this time.' When Bradman wrote his book after his return to Australia he made the following comment, 'I am not gloating over the fact that on this day I made 252 not out, but I did feel that if this innings had not put me on my feet as far as Mr Fender was concerned, I at least felt satisfied.'

Bradman's 252 not out against Surrey (the rest of the match was washed out, so Bradman did not get a chance to continue his innings) was a triumph achieved at Fender's expense. Fender had been made to look foolish. Not only did he fail to get Bradman out, but, worse, he failed hopelessly at trying to contain him. Douglas Jardine was on the field that day and, like the rest of the Surrey players, was no doubt made to do a lot of running about by Bradman. He, too, was probably aware of the personal motive behind Bradman's

assault on the bowling, and he must have felt for his
friend and captain, Fender, in his predicament. It is
even possible that Jardine conceived a dislike of the
young Australian during this innings. Jardine had an
aversion to Australians generally, and Bradman, revel-
ling in his own supremacy, might well have seemed to
Jardine the most unpalatable kind of Australian of all.
Although some of the men who played under Jardine
dispute this, there is little doubt that Jardine felt a
special antipathy towards Bradman. It would be possible to come to this conclusion solely on the basis of
Jardine's writing. He was rarely prepared to concede
Bradman anything, not even that bodyline was
developed specifically as a means of countering Bradman's ability to win matches with his own bat. But we
know that to be true.

It is possible, too, that it was Bradman's innings
against Surrey which first set Jardine's mind working
on the problem of how he might be fettered. Jardine
had seen him score a few centuries in Australia in
1928–29, but this was his first experience of the Bradman run-making machine operating at full blast, and
he could not have helped but be impressed. Jardine
had a fine cricket brain and, even if at this stage he did
not foresee himself captaining a team against the
Australians, it would have been natural for him to
take an academic interest in the question to which
every leading bowler in England was soon addressing
himself: how could the Australian Samson be stripped
of his strength?

2
Jardine

It has been said of Douglas Jardine that he was a weak man who forced himself to be a strong one. If this were true, it would explain the many contradictions of personality observed by all who were close to him. On the one hand, he seemed shy, sensitive, highly strung; on the other, harsh, inflexible, fiercely determined. He was so nervous while waiting to bat that he sometimes could not bear to watch the play and, during the bodyline Tests, went so far as to open the batting to spare himself the anxiety of sitting with his pads on. Yet he was fearless to the point of deliberately inviting the anger of Australian crowds, as he did when he positioned himself on one occasion close to the boundary where the barrackers were noisiest. He could be extremely kind. Jardine's vice-captain in 1932–33, Bob Wyatt, tells of meeting Jardine outside the Old Trafford ground in Manchester in the late 1940s. Wyatt had a car and offered Jardine a lift to where he was staying, which Jardine accepted only after persuasion. Jardine directed Wyatt to one of Manchester's poorer districts but remained evasive about his precise destination, eventually asking to be dropped at the next corner. It was only when Wyatt insisted on driving him all the way that Jardine revealed he was staying at the home of an old Army nurse who had been kind to him in hospital during the Second World War. 'The old girl is in a bad way financially,' Jardine confessed to Wyatt, 'and I'm going there as a PG [paying guest].' Wyatt says, 'He could have stayed at the best hotel in Manchester with his friends but he was doing some old nurse a good turn instead and didn't want anyone to know about it.' On other occasions, he could appear wholly indifferent to the feelings of others, including his own players. Australians found him off-hand and abrasive, at least in his playing days. There was nothing so clear about Jardine's personality as its complexity.

Douglas Jardine came from a Scottish colonial family which was connected, though distantly, with the Jardines of Jardine Matheson, the Hong Kong-based trading company, and with the Jardine brothers, Frank and Alec, the Cape York pioneers who established a cattle station on the peninsula in the 1860s. It was also a family of lawyers. Douglas's grandfather, William Jardine, a barrister, served in India and for a time was Acting Judge of the Allahabad High Court. Douglas's Indian-born father, Malcolm, commonly known as M. R. Jardine, studied law at Oxford and returned to India to practise as a barrister. M. R. Jardine was an outstanding cricketer, winning a Blue for cricket in his first year at Oxford and captaining the Oxford team in his third. He played briefly for Middlesex, but his first-class career was cut short by his early return to India. We may surmise that, in his son's cricket career, M. R. Jardine saw the fulfilment of his own unfulfilled ambitions.

Jardine was an only child, so his first years in India must have been solitary ones. Arthur Mailey wrote that he had once been told by M. R. Jardine, 'As a boy we could never understand Douglas. He seemed so distant and lonely. He seldom played with the other boys.' It does seem strange that M. R. Jardine should have confided this to an Australian cricketer he hardly knew, but, assuming Mailey remembered the remark accurately, it must be considered a most revealing one. When Jardine was still a small boy, his parents sent him to a preparatory school in England called Horris Hill. One story has been recorded of Jardine at Horris Hill, which shows that in his case the boy was truly the father of the man. According to R. C. Robertson–Glasgow's account of it, young Jardine politely but firmly corrected his master on a point of cricket technique, citing in his support a quotation from C. B. Fry's book, *Batsmanship*. From Horris Hill, Jardine advanced to the exclusive public school, Winchester, where he shone as a cricketer but where he also gained a reputation for being 'difficult', a description often applied to Jardine by people who knew him. His cricket coach at Winchester was a Yorkshire player named Rockley Wilson, one of the characters of English cricket in the first half of the century. It was Wilson who made the much-quoted remark about Jardine in 1931 when he was named captain of England: 'Well, we shall win the Ashes – but we may lose a Dominion.' (There are several versions of the Wilson remark – this is E. W. Swanton's.) The remark was remembered two years later when relations between England and Australia were soured by Jardine's bodyline.

There can be no doubt about the young Jardine's excellence as a cricketer. R. C. Robertson–Glasgow played against him in his last two years of school and then with him at Oxford. He wrote:

'Douglas Jardine, at 19 years, was the completest young batsman I have seen, both in method and temperament . . . Tall and well-proportioned, he had ever been the perfect example of the orthodox English style. His off-driving, which in Test matches against Australia he was apt to deny himself, was then free and strong, and the bowler who attacked his leg stump was but wasting himself in vanity. But where

Jardine excelled was in his back stroke. It was professional, near to perfect.'

Jardine's orthodoxy was such that strokes he demonstrated for the camera when he was in his prime now look stilted, almost affected. Aided by a long reach – he was 6' 2" (188 cm) tall – he had an extremely tight defence, and defence was the basis of his game. Neville Cardus wrote of him, 'If it is necessary for victory's sake to bat an hour and make no runs – very well, then, Jardine will enjoy the grind of it all; the crowd can perish of boredom.'

Jardine was captain of Winchester's cricket team, and it seems his captaincy was admired. The cricket historian H. S. Altham, who was a master at Winchester, declared he was one of the best schoolboy captains he ever knew. Yet he was never made captain of Oxford, as his father had been, although his leadership qualities must have been apparent to all. E. W. Swanton suggested that Jardine did not get the captaincy because of his 'sardonic reserve'. According to a contemporary of Jardine, a fellow amateur, it was because he was considered a 'difficult person'. One way or another, Jardine must have alienated people at Oxford by his manner. By now, perhaps, he had encased himself within that flint-hard shell, which for the rest of his life only a few intimates penetrated with ease. His daughter, Mrs Fianach Lawry, says that Jardine's 'iron side', as she calls it, was essentially a shield for his shyness. Mrs Lawry believes her father was conditioned by his upbringing to be the kind of man he was. The early years he spent at school in England, far from his parents in India (they did not return to England until 1916), might easily have had the effect of turning a naturally introverted boy further in upon

himself. Then came Winchester, with its code of the
stiff upper lip. Mrs Lawry says:

> 'I think a lot went on underneath the surface that didn't
> necessarily come out, for this is the way Winchester worked
> in those days. The silences and the things he didn't say
> perhaps made people think he was a hard man. The idea was
> not to let anyone see that you were hurt or upset. He was
> bad at communicating in today's terms, but there again we're
> back in Winchester. I think Winchester has a lot to answer
> for.'

The year 1921 was an important one in English cricket,
for an Australian team was in the country that year for
the first time since the war, a most cheering symbol of
the return to normalcy. Jardine was in the Oxford
team that year, so the visit by the Australians was
specially important for him. To do well against the
Australians when they came to Oxford, particularly so
strong an Australian side as Warwick Armstrong's in
1921, would have been quite an achievement for a
twenty-year-old undergraduate. Jardine did very well;
indeed, he almost had a triumph. He was 94 not out
when the match ended and would no doubt have got
his century if the match had not been shortened, at the
prior request of the Australians, from three days to
two. Arthur Mailey was in that Australian team, and
many years later he recorded his first impression then
of Douglas Jardine:

> 'He never spoke to any of the Australians, and as far as I
> know he seldom mixed with any of his own team. He was so
> withdrawn it seemed an effort for him to whisper, "Two legs,
> please," to the umpire when he came in to bat. He drew my
> notice more than any other (Oxford) player mainly because
> his features were so like a caricature. He had a hawk-
> like face with very high cheekbones, slanting eyes and the
> immobility of an Aztec.'

When Jack Fingleton came to write *Cricket Crisis*, his inspired account of the bodyline controversy, he made special mention of Oxford's match against the Australians in 1921. Fingleton speculated that the seeds of the ill-feeling Jardine later bore Australians may have been sown during that match. The Australians had asked for the match to be shortened to two days to allow themselves a rest day before the approaching Test, and Oxford graciously had agreed. Under such circumstances, Fingleton said, the Australians might easily have exerted themselves to play an extra over or two, or made some other kind of gesture, to enable the young Oxford batsman to reach his century. But there was no gesture from the Australians, the match ended on time and Jardine was left, perhaps, to brood in disappointment. Fingleton wondered whether Jardine might not always have remembered this first encounter with Australian cricketers and whether, because of it, he was never afterwards prepared to show them any mercy.

Douglas Jardine was in the strong MCC side which toured Australia under Percy Chapman in 1928–29. He began in fine fashion, scoring a century in each of his first three matches, and although he never ran hot like this again during the tour he did perform with reasonable consistency in the Tests, twice scoring in the sixties and once, in the fourth Test, failing by only two runs to get a century. But from the start, or at least almost from the start, Jardine decided he did not like Australians, and a great many Australians decided they did not like him. This mutual antipathy in 1928–29 deserves close examination, for there is no doubt that it had a bearing, perhaps an important bearing, on what happened four years later. The Australians' dislike of Jardine is easy enough to understand, even if not so easy to excuse. Jardine would have made himself unpopular with them by his slow batting in any case, but, as all his contemporaries seem to agree, he was a butt for Australian barrackers that summer mainly because of the kind of man he was. Nobody has explained this better than Jack Fingleton in the following passage in *Cricket Crisis*:

> 'As he strode out to bat, a tall, angular acidulated and seemingly aloof Englishman, with a gaudy cap rampant and a silk handkerchief knotted around his throat, he walked into the vision of many Australians as the very personification of the old school tie . . . They considered him a barracking gift from the gods.'

Jardine seems to have worn his tri-coloured Harlequin cap frequently in 1928–29; if one can judge from photographs, he wore it more often then than he did four years later. Harlequin caps were worn as badges of honour by men who had played for Oxford, and it does appear that Jardine was genuinely sensitive about his. Arthur Mailey was a cricket writer in 1928–29 and saw a lot of Jardine on tour. Mailey saw a lot of significance in the cap, for it was his belief that Jardine resented Australians poking fun at it more deeply than he did all the other insults he received. The barrackers were not the only Australians who did this, incidentally. The press made jokes about it in 1928–29, too, and Mailey believed this was the cause of Jardine's dislike of Australian journalists, which so affected his relations with the press in 1932–33.

The following is a personal recollection by C. R. Ashford, a cricketer from the Upper Hunter area who played against the Englishmen in a regional match in 1932–33. Mr Ashford writes:

'In the 1928–29 season one of, if not the, most objectionable remarks I ever heard on a cricket ground was made to Jardine in Sydney. I had been seated in the Sheridan Stand and a few minutes before stumps I moved down to the fence where Jardine was fielding at fine leg. A very dirty, smelly newspaper-seller had just sold his last paper. He moved to the fence, leant over it and touched Jardine on the shoulder and said, "Hey, Jardine – I'd like your nose full of rum."'

No doubt there were many more incidents of this kind that summer.

John Arlott, who got to know Jardine well after the war, believes that in his playing days Jardine tended to equate Australians as a whole with Australian barrackers. 'And Australian barrackers disgusted him,' Arlott says. Perhaps his colonial background conditioned him to view Australians in a certain light. This would help explain the unpleasant exchange he had with the Australian Test cricketer Hunter (Stork) Hendry at the start of the 1928–29 tour. Hendry played for Victoria in the second match of the tour, which was one of the matches in which Jardine made a hundred. The Melbourne crowd watched without protest while Jardine crept towards his century, but when he passed that mark and still made no attempt to step up the scoring rate the crowd became impatient. 'They really got at him – they started to give him hell,' Hendry says. Hendry had gone out of his way to congratulate Jardine on reaching his century – Hendry had, and still has, great admiration for his technique – and now that the barrackers were on his back he made a light-hearted observation about them, as if to tell Jardine not to let them bother him. 'I was fielding in slips only a yard or two from him,' Hendry says. 'I said to him, "I hear the wolves are out", meaning the crowd. With that he turned around and said Australians were just

bloody mongrels, and he obviously meant me included.
I said, "If that's your opinion you can go to buggery."
He was the only person I ever swore at on a cricket
field.' Asked if Jardine had actually said 'mongrels',
Hendry replied, 'He may not have used that word, but
that was his meaning.'

Among Jardine's team-mates that summer was the
young Nottinghamshire fast bowler Harold Larwood,
who like Jardine was on his first tour of Australia.
Born in November 1904, Larwood was the son of a
coal-miner and grew up in a coal-mining village. He
left school at thirteen and got an above-ground job at
the local mine, and at fourteen, the minimum age, he
became a pit boy, working below ground. It must have
been a grim life for someone so young, but Larwood
did have one escape from it – cricket. He had played
the game since he was a small boy, sometimes in the
streets of his village, Nuncargate, and it seems he
had always been a fast bowler. Even after he became a
pit boy, he often played cricket in the late afternoon
after he had finished a full day's work. 'Down the
mine I dreamed of cricket,' Larwood wrote long afterwards. 'I bowled imaginary balls in the dark; I sent the
stumps spinning and heard them rattling in the tunnels.'
At fifteen he was short and slightly built but was
judged good enough to play in a men's team as a fast
bowler.

In those early years cricket was for Larwood a
temporary relief from the drudgery of the mine. In
1923, when he was eighteen, cricket became the means
of his deliverance from it. On the strength of his
performances for the Nuncargate team, Larwood was
given a trial in the nets by the Nottinghamshire County
Cricket Club at Trent Bridge, and he impressed the

club's officials enough to be offered a job as a professional. This did not mean he immediately had a place in the county team; at first he did a variety of menial jobs about the Trent Bridge ground, including cleaning the boots of visiting players. In 1925, however, he became a regular member of the Notts county side and in 1926, when the Australians were touring England, he played his first Test. As Larwood himself observed, 'The pony pit boy had come a long way.'

Larwood was a complex character. Quiet, introverted and, by his own admission, extremely shy, he could also be stubborn and quick to anger. Most definitely, he was not one to be pushed around. On the field, there was in him a strong streak of aggression, and in any analysis of the bodyline story it would be very wrong to view Larwood, as some have viewed him, as merely the tool of an unscrupulous captain. When Larwood came to bowl bodyline for Jardine, he did it not only willingly but with apparent fervour. One Australian who played against Larwood believes it was when he was on the field with a cricket ball in his hand that Larwood expressed his manhood most fully and confidently.

Larwood was 5' 7½" (171 cm) tall, which was short for a bowler of express pace, but he was of strong and fairly broad build. His bowling action, as recorded on newsreel film, was marvellous to behold. At the end of a beautifully rhythmic and relaxed approach to the wicket, his left arm and left knee were raised high together and were held there, in fixed pose, for a fleeting moment while he skimmed across the bowling crease on his right instep. It was in this momentary pause during his delivery stride that Larwood seemed to gather himself for the final, violent propulsion of the ball. In his book, *The Larwood Story*, Larwood says that after he joined Notts it took three years of intensive coaching and practice to perfect his run to the wicket and bowling action. He suggests that his magnificent action was really the creation of one of his Nottinghamshire coaches, Jimmy Iremonger, but he was surely not giving due credit here to his own natural ability. Only an athlete who was supremely co-ordinated and innately graceful could have bowled the way Larwood bowled.

In 1928–29, on the hard and true Australian wickets, Larwood achieved only moderate success. Everyone agreed he was a bowler of exceptional pace, but pace by itself was not sufficient to worry the Australian batsmen. In the second Test a rising ball from Larwood broke the hand of the Australian opener Bill Ponsford on the first day, but in the second innings the Australian batsmen Bill Woodfull and Hunter Hendry came together in a long partnership which eventually put on 215 for the second wicket. In vain did Larwood try to get life from the pitch, and Hendry found him so easy to handle that he was able to pull shorter balls from outside the off stump. Eventually, in desperation, Larwood resorted to a highly novel form of attack. It received only a passing mention in the press, but in the light of events four years later it was a profoundly interesting experiment. This is one newspaper's account of it:

'Undoubtedly the English bowling was mastered. Larwood was forced to change his tactics. At one stage he adopted a short-leg theory field, pitching his deliveries short, and bumping them at the batsman. He did not succeed, and later reverted to the orthodox deployment.'

What we seem to have here is bodyline in embryo form. Note that the writer says Larwood was bouncing

the ball *at* the batsman. This is precisely what Larwood
was accused of doing in 1932–33, and, moreover, he
was doing it here with a leg-theory field. Whose idea
was it to employ such tactics? Was it the England
captain's, or some other fieldsman's, or Larwood's?
The press report suggests it was Larwood's, but we
cannot tell for sure. If it was Larwood's idea, did he
think of it there and then, or was it a strategy worked
out beforehand? These questions must intrigue anyone
trying to trace the bodyline story.

In 1928–29 England had no need to use unorthodox
tactics – it won the series comfortably enough using
orthodox ones. England won the first four Tests, two
of them by big margins, and lost the fifth. The result
was a fair measure of England's superiority, but already
that superiority was in danger. In the 1928–29 series
Don Bradman made his first appearance in international cricket. He failed in the first Test and was
made twelfth man for the second, but he scored centuries in the third and fifth Tests and ended the series
with an average of 66.86. The Englishmen could not
have guessed this at the time, but Bradman's arrival
had radically changed the balance of strength between
the two countries. With Bradman, Australia would be
unbeatable. If England wanted to defeat Australia, it
would have to devise some means, fair or foul, of
curbing him.

3
Captain of England

Bradman's sensational scoring in 1930 left England's cricket world in a state of discomposure. Nobody doubted that he was largely responsible for Australia's 2–1 victory in the Tests and its consequent recovery of the Ashes. Pelham Warner, a man of influence in English cricket, wrote, 'The difference between the two elevens was little. Bradman was England's trouble; had he been content with scores of 120 or 150, all would have been well, but he smashed through our defences with his stupendous two hundreds and three hundreds.' There seemed little hope for England in future contests with Australia, so long as the Australian side included Bradman. Bradman was only twenty-two, and it was quite possible that England's bowlers had not yet seen the worst of him. Warner wondered about this himself after the 1930 tour. 'What is his future?' he wrote. 'Will he one day play an innings of 600 or 700, and put the aggregate of Grace and Hobbs, and their numbers of centuries, in the shade?' For England's sake, some means had to be found to prevent this happening.

In 1931 England's trouble became, in a sense, Warner's trouble. At the beginning of that year he was appointed chairman of a new England selection committee consisting of himself, Percy Perrin and Tommy Higson. Ostensibly, the selectors' duty was to choose teams for the Tests against New Zealand in 1931 and against India in 1932, but, as Warner later described it, 'the real object was to build up a side for the

Australian tour' of 1932–33. It was for Warner a fateful appointment, for thereafter he was swept along by the flow of events to the very centre of the bodyline controversy, and nobody disliked controversy more than Pelham Warner. He was a quietly spoken, genteel, conservative man, who believed fervently in the value of tradition. 'This modern scoffing at tradition is a product of super-democracy,' he once told an Australian journalist. 'Tradition is a hell of a good thing. It's what takes a regiment through hell. Good God, you fellows out in Australia have a great tradition. What fighters you are!' He counted cricket among the noblest of traditions. 'Wherever cricket has become popular it has been a beneficial influence,' he said. 'Next to the Throne, cricket is the greatest link in the Empire.'

Warner had a background strangely similar to Jardine's. He was born abroad, in Trinidad in October 1873, and, like Jardine, his father was a colonial lawyer who served as Trinidad's Attorney-General. Warner took to cricket at an early age. Legend has it that he used to play the game before breakfast in his nightshirt on a marble gallery at his father's home, a most appealing scene. A black servant boy named Humming Bird used to bowl to him, and young Warner once hit a ball through a window, incurring only a mild reprimand from his father. Unlike Jardine, Warner came from a large family. His father, Charles, had eighteen children, the last twelve of them by his second wife, Warner's mother. One of his brothers is said to have died of sunstroke after playing cricket, which suggests that Pelham was not the only Warner dedicated to the game. Charles Warner died when Pelham was thirteen, and the family returned to England. Warner went to Rugby school and then, also like Jardine, to Oxford, to study law, playing cricket for the university team in 1895 and 1896.

After Oxford, he continued his cricket career with Middlesex, and in 1903, although he had never played a Test, he was chosen to captain the England team touring Australia the following summer. There were crowd disturbances at the Tests in 1903–04, particularly at the Sydney Cricket Ground, where spectators on the Hill were angered by several umpiring decisions. Warner reported in a newspaper article that barrackers at Sydney accused him of bribing the umpires. 'They are a lovely crowd in Sydney,' Warner said in a despatch to the *Westminster Gazette*, 'and anyone who has taken part in a Test match here may consider himself thoroughly salted, and fit to play before an audience from the infernal regions.' Warner returned to Australia as captain in 1911–12, but became ill at the start of the tour and did not lead England in any of the Tests. He played first-class cricket for Middlesex until 1920, when he was nearly forty-seven, but even then he could not give the game up. Retirement merely allowed him to devote more time to the affairs of the MCC, in which he soon became influential.

Although Warner had been bald since his university days, he had a fresh, pink complexion which made him look younger than his years. In his playing days he had a habit of taking off his cap and stroking his scalp, which used to surprise spectators who did not know he was bald, because he looked so youthful in his cap. He gave some Australians who met him a faint impression of physical frailty, which somehow seemed in keeping with the mildness of his personality. It does not seem there was anybody who knew Warner who did not like him. He was a man of gentle nature

and gentlemanly manner. His was not a strong character, at least not nearly so strong as Douglas Jardine's,
a fact which was to have important consequences in
1932–33.

Warner and his co-selectors chose Jardine to lead
England against New Zealand in 1931. It was certainly
not an automatic choice, for it does not seem that
Jardine had captained a side, regularly anyway, since
he left Winchester and, moreover, he played cricket
only intermittently since the 1928–29 tour of Australia.
But Warner personally was impressed by Jardine, both
as a cricketer and as a student of the game, and he
appears to have promoted Jardine's cause himself.
Warner had known and admired Jardine's father, so
he would have been well disposed to Jardine to begin
with. Writing some years later about Jardine's elev-
ation to the captaincy, Warner recalled his association
with Jardine's father in the following comment:

> 'When in 1931 I came into closer contact with his son, I
> realized – it was easy to do – that here was a man who was a
> thorough student of the game of cricket, keen and competent,
> one who had thought much and pondered deeply over the
> tactics and strategy of the game and, incidentally, a stern
> critic of his own cricketing abilities. The coming tour appeared
> to him in the light of a crusade, and it was certain that he
> would put his whole soul and endeavour into the work in
> front of him. Backed by my colleagues, I recommended him
> to the MCC committee in an appreciation of the situation
> which is, no doubt, in the archives at Lord's.'

This is revealing and yet confusing. When Warner
speaks of recommending Jardine for the captaincy, it
is unclear whether he refers to the captaincy in 1931,
when the New Zealanders were in England, or in
1932–33, the season of the bodyline Tests. The probability is he was referring to the former, but then what

are we to make of the statement that Jardine viewed
the coming tour of Australia in the light of a crusade?
Does it mean that Jardine, early in 1931, was looking
beyond the Tests of 1931 and 1932 to the tour of
Australia? It may have been so; the selectors, as we
have seen, were looking as far ahead as that. In any
case, the word 'crusade' is surely a significant one. It
implies Jardine saw the mission ahead as a very special
one: the Ashes had to be recovered and Don Bradman
had to be subdued. No captain of England had faced a
tougher challenge than that.

Yet there is evidence that Jardine was reluctant
initially to accept the captaincy and had to be persuaded to do so by his father, M. R. Jardine. In his
biography of Bradman, Irving Rosenwater says that,
according to Jardine's cousin, Jardine changed his mind
after being appointed captain for the 1932–33 tour and
told Warner that he would not be available. Warner
turned for help to M. R. Jardine, who is supposed to
have said, 'I'll have a word with the boy.' Edward
Docker tells a similar story in his book about the
bodyline series, reporting M. R. Jardine as saying to
Warner, 'Don't worry. I'll speak to the boy.' In
Docker's version, however, Jardine declined to accept
the captaincy for the Tests against New Zealand in
1931, not the tour of Australia.

Obviously, something of the kind occurred, which
raises the question: why would a man who at one
moment viewed the coming tour of Australia in the
light of a crusade be reluctant at another to accept the
captaincy? Perhaps it was for professional reasons:
Jardine had given his work priority over his cricket
many times before. Perhaps, too, it was because com-
plications had arisen in his romantic life. In 1930
Jardine had become engaged to a Harrow girl, but the

engagement was broken off before he led the MCC team to Australia in 1932. If cricket did come between Jardine and his fiancée, it would not have been the first time this kind of thing had happened, nor the last.

Jardine led England to victory over New Zealand in 1931, impressing people generally by his performance as captain. Towards the end of January 1932, the British newspaper *News of the World* announced that it was in a position to state that Douglas Jardine would captain the MCC side in Australia at the end of the year. In March the *Daily Herald* reported that Jardine had been 'virtually selected' to lead the team to Australia. In fact, Jardine's appointment was not announced officially until July that year, although we may deduce from the press reports that the MCC had all but settled on him for the job six months before. There may have been a clue to the MCC's intentions in the Surrey Club's decision in February to dismiss Percy Fender as county captain. At the time the London press believed the Surrey Club had acted under pressure from the MCC, which was said to want Jardine to captain Surrey for a season before leading the MCC in Australia. Whether or not this was true, Jardine did replace Fender as captain of Surrey in 1932.

Warner was approached by the MCC to go on the Australian tour as manager in February 1932. Warner asked for time to consider the invitation and spent 'many a restless night' before accepting it. Did he, we may wonder, have an inkling of the troubles ahead? Later, the MCC decided to send a second manager, R. C. N. Palairet, the brother of the renowned batting stylist, Lionel Palairet. Warner and Palairet had been at Oriel College, Oxford, together, so they knew each other well. The arrangement between them, as outsiders understood it, was that Warner would perform the social duties of tour manager and Palariet would look after the bookkeeping. The MCC's decision to send joint managers was a surprise, and some people were inclined later to see something sinister in it. In *Cricket Crisis*, Jack Fingleton quoted the pre-war English bowler Frank Foster as saying, 'In the whole history of cricket there have never previously been two managers sent to Australia with an English Eleven. Warner was sent to keep the peace.' The fact that Warner had been approached about the job as early as February must rule out the possibility that the MCC knew of Jardìne's intentions in detail when it asked Warner to go. It is quite possible, though, that the MCC guessed Jardine was bound to ruffle feathers in Australia by one means or another and that it considered Warner an ideal man to smooth the feathers down.

Jardine's appointment as captain of the team to tour Australia in 1932–33 was a break in tradition, and one that seems to have been widely welcomed in English cricket circles. Many Englishmen felt it was high time their cricketers stood up to the Australians. The Australians had always played the game hard, they believed, while English cricketers, led by amateur captains, had concerned themselves with being good sportsmen. The Australians played to win matches; the English played to win friends. With Jardine in command, things would be different. The Australians would no longer have things all their own way. Jardine would give them as good as, if not better than, the Englishmen got.

4

A Plan is Born

Bodyline was not Jardine's creation, it was his adaptation. Essentially, bodyline was an aggravated form of leg-theory bowling, and leg-theory bowling had been used from time to time for fifty years at least. Tom Horan of Victoria bowled it in a NSW–Victoria match in Sydney in February 1882, a match in which Billy Murdoch made 321. Pelham Warner had a leg-theory bowler in the team he led in Australia in 1903–04 – George Hirst, a fastish left-hander. A diagram published by the Sydney sporting journal, *Referee*, during the tour shows that Hirst bowled to a field curiously like the one deployed by Jardine for Larwood. There was an inner ring of three short-legs and a silly mid-on, and two men near the boundary on the leg-side. Moreover, the diagram shows that Hirst bowled around the wicket, angling his deliveries into the right-handed batsman and forcing him to play to the on-side. The object was to get the batsman to edge or mis-hit a catch to one of the short-legs, or to hook a catch to one of the two men in the deep. There was another leg-theory bowler in the team which Warner brought to Australia in 1911–12 – Frank Foster, also a fastish left-hander. Like Hirst, Foster bowled around the wicket to a field consisting of an inner cordon of short-legs and two men in the deep on the legside. There is a photograph of him bowling leg-theory to Victor Trumper in the fourth Test at Melbourne. He had one slip on the off-side, a leg-slip, and two fieldsmen about twenty metres from the bat, one forward and the other backward of square leg. Foster was extremely successful in the Tests that summer, and it is surprising he did not have more imitators. After the war, leg-theory methods continued to be employed by a handful of bowlers, most notably Fred Root of Worcestershire and Jack Scott of New South Wales, the second of whom experimented with them briefly and unsuccessfully in the mid–1920s. Until 1932 leg-theory remained an eccentric, essentially negative and generally unsuccessful method of bowling.

Bodyline evolved from these various kinds of leg-theory bowling. It was, if you like, at the top of leg-theory's evolutionary tree. But (to continue this analogy) it was related to earlier varieties of leg-theory only in the way that man is related to the other primates: there were certain external similarities but a vast difference in spirit. Bodyline had two elements: a special kind of bowling and a special kind of field setting, each of them wholly dependent on the other. The bowling consisted of fast, short-pitched deliveries directed straight at the batsman, which meant that a high proportion of them bounced at the batsman's hip, shoulder and head. The bodyline field consisted, typically, of a cordon of five closer fieldsmen extending from leg-slip to silly mid-on and another two fieldsmen near the long-leg boundary. Such an arrangement meant there could be only two fieldsmen on the off-side of the wicket. Sometimes, the number of fieldsmen in the inner cordon was increased to six. The theory was that the batsman would not only be forced to play the ball if it were directed straight at his body, but he would be forced to play it towards the leg-side cordon, where sooner or later a catch would result. If he tried to hook the ball over the cordon, he ran the risk of being caught by one of the two men in the deep. As leg-theory bowlers had discovered many years previously, best results were obtained when the bowler was able to angle the ball into the batsman. The Australians considered bodyline bowling unfair because, as they saw it, intimidation was the essence of it. They held that it relied on the fear of injury it produced in batsmen. Jack Fingleton wrote: 'Bodyline demanded an occasional hit or near miss. It was part of the plan and inherent in its nature.'

Bodyline, then, was a leg-theory attack which incorporated persistent, short-pitched bowling. Someone with a flair for conciseness defined bodyline as leg-theory with plenty of bouncers, which is accurate as far as it goes. Les Ames, who kept wickets for England in every bodyline Test, was quoted in a *Wisden Cricket Monthly* article in 1982 as saying that, typically, there would be four bouncers in an eight-ball over. This contravened no cricket law at the time, which is the reason the umpires in 1932–33 were powerless to act, even if they had wanted to.

Over the years several men have been given the credit, or blame, for 'inventing' bodyline. Percy Fender was one. Another was Arthur Carr, the captain of Nottinghamshire. The evidence suggests, however, that it was Jardine, and Jardine alone, who conceived the idea of it and developed it into a workable strategy. What gave him the inspiration? To answer this question, we must examine again bodyline's primary purpose. In a book he wrote about the 1932–33 tour, *In Quest of the Ashes*, Jardine made the following statement:

'I am sorry to disappoint anyone who has imagined that the leg-theory was evolved with the help of midnight oil and iced towels, simply and solely for the purpose of combating

Bradman's effectiveness as a scoring machine. However highly Bradman may have been rated, this view is an exaggeration.'

It seems Jardine was intent here on denying Bradman a back-handed compliment for being so masterful that England had to devise an entirely new method of attack to deal with him. In fact, there does not seem to have been one other cricketer on either side in that Test series who was not convinced that bodyline was designed specifically to counter Bradman.

Which leads us to the next question: why should Jardine have believed that bodyline might be specially effective against Bradman? Jardine provided his own explanation for this. He wrote, 'Though I did not take part in the last Test match against Australia at the Oval in 1930, I have been told on all sides that Bradman's innings, impressive though it was in the number of runs scored, was far from convincing on the leg stump whilst there was any life in the wicket.' Jardine refers here to a period during Bradman's innings of 232 in the fifth Test in 1930 in which Larwood made the ball rear dangerously on a rain-affected pitch. This is Larwood's account of what happened, contained in his book, *The Larwood Story:*

'Don didn't like the balls rising on his body. He was hit once or twice but the real significance in his play during the duel was that he kept drawing away. It wasn't all that obvious to me at first because I was mainly concerned with getting balls up off a length, but I began to notice that he flinched. Others saw it too and talked about it after the match. I thought Bradman was a bit frightened of the ball that got up sharply.'

Only Bradman himself can say for sure whether he was in discomfort against Larwood that day, and he has insisted that he was not. In his book *Farewell to*

Cricket he was able to cite various newspaper reports of his innings, which praised him for standing up gamely to extremely hostile bowling on a most malevolent pitch. The important thing, however, is that several of the English players *believed* Bradman was unhappy against the rising deliveries. Gubby Allen, an opponent of bodyline and a friend of Bradman's, is 'pretty sure' he can remember English players discussing it at the time.

Jardine, who apparently was not there to see for himself, says he was told 'on all sides' later about Bradman's alleged weakness. This may have been some time later, of course, perhaps after he knew he was to captain the MCC in Australia. It is certain that from the moment he learned he was to be captain, and he may have learned of it unofficially quite early in 1932, he would have cast about anxiously for some novel means of stifling Bradman's scoring. It would have been apparent to him that any conventional form of attack was sure to fail; the only uncertainty would be how many double centuries Bradman would score. If Jardine and other Englishmen had entertained any hopes that Bradman would not be able to maintain his astonishing rate of run-making, those hopes would certainly have been abandoned by 1932. Since his triumphs in England in 1930, Bradman had played two seasons of Test and Sheffield Shield cricket in Australia. In 1930–31, when the West Indians were in Australia, he made a handful of moderate scores to begin with, but in his last twelve innings that season he peeled off three double centuries and two centuries. In 1931–32 he batted only thirteen times but scored three double centuries and four centuries. His average in four Tests against the South Africans that season was 201.5. It would have been clear to Jardine, who must have been following Bradman's career with interest, that Bradman was scoring a century every second time he went to the wicket and that one in two of those centuries became a double century. Unless some means could be found to put an end to this, Jardine might find himself leading a side in Australia whose principal function, as viewed by the Australian public, was to provide Don Bradman with the opportunity of performing more fantastic feats of batsmanship. Such a prospect would not have appealed to Jardine.

It is impossible to say when the bodyline plan started to take shape in Jardine's mind, but it can be said with hindsight that the composition of the MCC touring side, announced in late July, probably gave the first clue to his intentions. There were three fast bowlers in it – Larwood, Bill Voce and Gubby Allen – and a fourth, Bill Bowes, was added to the touring party later. Gubby Allen does not believe that this was of itself significant; he thinks the selectors simply picked the best bowlers, and it so happened that a larger proportion than normal of those bowlers were fast bowlers. On the other hand, Larwood was sure he and the other fast bowlers were chosen for a purpose. 'The members of the MCC selection committee must have been fully aware that the Australians in 1932 were in for a further taste of leg-theory,' he wrote. 'There had never been four speed merchants sent to Australia before.' In Australia, Bradman himself was suspicious. 'When the personnel of the English team to tour Australia in 1932–33 was announced, I foresaw the possibility of trouble because of the abnormal selection of four fast bowlers . . .,' he wrote. 'It seemed obvious that we were to be subjected to a battery of fast bowling, although the precise nature of it could not, at that stage, have been foreseen.' Bradman probably guessed, too, that he was meant to be the battery's main target. Not long after Jardine's men arrived in Australia, Bradman told Jack Fingleton, while playing golf, that he believed the Englishmen thought he could be daunted by pace. 'Bradman knew then what was up the English sleeve,' Fingleton said. Others had already come to the same conclusion. Writing in the *Sydney Morning Herald* while the English team was still sailing to Australia, the former NSW player E. L. Waddy said, 'The English selectors seem to have concentrated on the thought of getting Bradman out, and apparently will work on shock tactics with their fast bowlers, and then bring on the slow bowlers.'

Jardine, as captain, had been co-opted to help the selectors choose the team. Pelham Warner wrote that Jardine worked with the selectors 'with great keenness and enthusiasm.' It is reasonable to assume that Jardine had a lot to do with the choice of four fast bowlers. It may even be that the four were chosen specifically at his request. By this time Jardine had sketched in his mind a plan to try to muzzle Bradman with fast leg-theory, and he would have regarded it as imperative to have the fast bowlers he needed to bowl it. What we do not know, and cannot really guess at, is the extent to which he confided his leg-theory plans to his fellow selectors. He must have told them something, if only to justify his demand for so many pace bowlers, and, as we have seen, Larwood for one believed the other selectors were 'fully aware' that Jardine intended to use leg-theory.

On the other hand, he could not have briefed his fellow selectors in detail, and he certainly could not have forewarned them about the controversial bowling methods he would eventually employ in Australia, because his planning was not nearly far enough advanced. But that said, the following statement by Jardine's daughter, Mrs Lawry, in a letter to *The Times* in 1975 deserves to be noted. 'Bodyline was not his [Jardine's] exclusive invention,' she said. 'It was discussed and fully approved of by the MCC, as the one way to beat Bradman before Jardine's team left England.' Jardine himself once hinted at MCC complicity. In an article in the *Cricketer* in 1980, Dennis Castle told of meeting Jardine during the war and of receiving from Jardine his own version of the bodyline story. 'He told me that in 1932 he felt that if Bradman had a weakness at all it was on the leg-stump and, with MCC agreement, he decided to make Larwood and Voce exploit it.' The words 'with MCC agreement' invite many kinds of speculation, yet it would be foolish to speculate about them here without a few hard facts to go by. Perhaps the archives at Lord's will one day supply them.

A few days after the team was announced Jardine decided to consult the two fast bowlers whom he hoped would be able to implement his leg-theory plans, Larwood and Voce. Two other people had a hand in arranging the meeting, Percy Fender and Arthur Carr, neither of whom, as it happened, was well disposed towards Australians. The severe barracking Fender received when he played in Australia in 1920–21 may have influenced his attitude in this respect; the crowds used to chant 'Please go home, Fender' in mockery of his initials, P. G. H. Some people, including Wally Hammond, claimed that it was Fender who first planted the bodyline idea in Jardine's mind, but Fender denied that this was so. However, he certainly helped Jardine formulate his leg-theory plan, once spending a weekend discussing tactics with him at Walton-on-Thames, where Jardine's father lived. Arthur Carr's dislike of

Australians was even less disguised than Jardine's. Carr was one of those who considered that Australian cricketers had been treated for too long with kid gloves. 'The game was never intended for namby-pambies,' he wrote later in defence of bodyline. The Australians had played the game hard themselves, so they ought to be the last to squeal if the Englishmen played hard, too. Carr once wrote:

> 'Cricket is a game, not a mixture of war and all-in-wrestling – a fact which I am very much afraid some people do not seem to realize. The Australians, for example . . . My own experience of Australians is that if they cannot win they will not stand to be beaten if they can help or avoid it. They will go to almost any length to dodge defeat . . . To the Australians cricket is a business almost pure and simple – a matter of money – and success is all that matters to them.'

These were hard words from a hard man. Carr had a lot in common with Jardine: both were gentleman cricketers, amateurs, but both had a tough, professional approach to the game. Carr was a strong-willed, temperamental character. As captain of Nottinghamshire, he had his two fast bowlers, Larwood and Voce, occasionally bowl a kind of fast leg-theory, which nevertheless stopped a good way short of bodyline, as early as 1931. At least that is when Carr himself said it was first used by the Notts attack, although it is on record that Voce bowled a form of leg-theory to the Australians in 1930. Thus, Carr was one of the most experienced practitioners in a field in which very few had any experience at all, and it was to him that Jardine turned for help and advice. When Notts came to London to play Surrey at the beginning of August 1932, Jardine took Carr, Larwood and Voce to dinner at the Piccadilly Hotel.

This meeting over a dinner table in the hotel's grill room has been writ large in bodyline lore. Although it was not, as it has sometimes been presented, the moment of bodyline's birth, it was the first time Jardine had allowed a glimpse of his offspring. The circumstances of the meeting are interesting. Carr said in his book, *Cricket With The Lid Off*, that there had been some whispering on the grapevine about a new bowling strategy and that Percy Fender was one of the first to know about it. This simply means, no doubt, that Fender was one of the first to be consulted by Jardine. Carr also said it was Fender who first approached him about going to dinner with Larwood and Voce as Jardine's guests. Fender and Carr were on friendly terms, and Jardine, who did not know Carr so well, obviously used Fender as a go-between. 'He [Fender] gave me the tip that Jardine wanted to learn more about my two bowlers, Larwood and Voce,' Carr said, which confirms again that Fender was in Jardine's confidence.

Carr and Larwood both wrote accounts of the dinner, Larwood's being much more detailed than Carr's, and both agreed that Jardine had sounded out the two bowlers on the idea of bowling leg-theory in Australia. According to Larwood, the discussion centred on how the leg-theory might be employed against Bradman. In Larwood's narrative, the following paragraph is the most revealing of all:

'At the dinner I didn't think we were breaking any fresh ground in deciding to bowl leg-theory to Bradman. At the same time I had no doubt of its purpose: we thought Don was frightened of sharp-rising balls and we reasoned that if he got a lot of them over the leg stump he would be put off his game and be intimidated, and eventually, having to direct his shots to the leg all the time, would give a catch to one of the onside fieldsmen.'

The word 'intimidated' seems to leap out of the page. What Larwood describes here is not leg-theory, but bodyline, almost fully fledged.

There was one more scene in the story to be played out before the team set sail for Australia. On 20 August, during Surrey's match against Yorkshire at the Oval, Bill Bowes of Yorkshire repeatedly bowled bouncers at Jack Hobbs, for part of the time with a strong leg-side field. They were surprising tactics to use against such a man as Hobbs, then only a few months off his fiftieth birthday, and Hobbs made it plain that he took exception to them, but the whole affair would have been forgotten within a week if Pelham Warner had not been there to see it and report on it for the *Morning Post*. His forthright criticism of Bowes's bowling was remembered, and frequently quoted, in Australia a few months later when, by contrast, Warner remained silent while Jardine was unleashing his bodyline attack. There is an interesting line of speculation on the matter in Edward Docker's *Bradman and the Bodyline Series*. Docker wondered whether Warner, by criticizing Bowes in the press, might not really have been signalling his disapproval of aggressive leg-theory to Jardine, for he ought to have had some idea by then that Jardine was thinking of using similar tactics in Australia. If Warner's comments were intended as a caution to Jardine, Jardine did not heed them. A few weeks later, quite possibly at Jardine's request, Bowes' name was added to the team list.

On paper, Jardine's team looked strong in all departments. In addition to the four fast bowlers, Larwood, Voce, Allen and Bowes, the team had a medium-pace bowler of outstanding reputation in Maurice Tate and a highly promising spin bowler in Hedley Verity. There were two wicketkeepers of the first rank, Les Ames and George Duckworth, and a most formidable array of batsmen – Wally Hammond, Herbert Sutcliffe, Maurice Leyland, Jardine himself, Eddie Paynter and the vice-captain, Bob Wyatt. The team sailed to Australia on the liner *Orontes*, sharing the voyage with the Australian Davis Cup team, and Jardine had a game of deck tennis with Cliff Sproule, watched by Harry Hopman, who acted as sports secretary for the voyage. Also on board were the two managers, Warner and Palairet, the team's Australian-born scorer and baggage man, Bill Ferguson, and a disappointingly lightweight press contingent. Only four journalists were sent to cover the tour – Jack Hobbs and his ghost writer Jack Ingham, representing the *London Star*, Bruce Harris of the *Evening Standard* and an Australian-born Reuters correspondent, Gilbert Mant. Harris was actually a tennis writer and, according to Mant, 'knew nothing whatever about cricket', but in the months ahead he was for many Englishmen the chief source of information about Jardine's controversial tactics. From the outset he had Jardine's confidence, and Jardine fed him information throughout the tour. An Australian journalist who shared the press box with Harris that summer remembers him as a 'lone wolf', a man who did not mix with the other cricket writers. The Australian journalist says Harris was virtually 'Jardine's offsider', so close was his association with the English captain. Harris's pro-Jardine reporting of the bodyline controversy has since been blamed for much of the ignorance about the issue which prevailed in England.

Up to this point, the development of Jardine's leg-theory plan is easy enough to follow. He observes the occasional use of fast leg-theory by bowlers such as

Voce and Larwood, and for some reason – perhaps because Bradman seemed disconcerted by Larwood's lifting deliveries at the Oval in 1930 – he hits upon the idea that this kind of bowling may be effective against Bradman. He consults the man he regards as the best tactician in England, Percy Fender, and Fender encourages him in the idea. Next, we are entitled to assume, he presses for the inclusion of a squad of fast bowlers in the touring party, and when the bowlers he wants are duly included he reveals his plan to the two best equipped to implement it, Larwood and Voce. Finally, he calls on the old leg-theory bowler Frank Foster to obtain details of the field placings he used in 1911–12.

Thereafter, however, Jardine's thinking is not at all easy to follow. Having developed his leg-theory plan thus far, he then seems to have deliberately shelved it for the time being. He discussed it in London with Larwood and Voce at the beginning of August, but, by all accounts, he did not mention it to another English player until he was all but forced to do so by Bowes in Adelaide more than three months later. Contrary to the belief of many, it appears Jardine did not discuss it with anyone else during the long boat trip to Australia. Larwood wrote that Jardine 'outlined his method of attack to the other fast bowlers' during the voyage, but the other fast bowlers, Allen and Bowes, insist today that he did not say a word to them about it. Since the recent resurgence of interest in the bodyline story, Allen has had lengthy discussions with three other survivors of Jardine's team, Wyatt, Ames and Freddie Brown. Having thus re-analysed the whole affair, this is how Allen views the question of bodyline's origins today:

'It is my belief that Douglas never formed a positive plan at that stage (before the team arrived in Australia). The whole thing was really how were they going to keep Bradman quiet. If they're going to tell me, as certain people have written, that the whole plan was made in England, I won't believe a word of it. You mean to tell me they had thrashed out bodyline, or what came to be known as bodyline, and nobody ever talked about it on the boat? We four will go to our graves saying we never once heard it mentioned on the boat. Now I can't believe that if this plot had really been hatched in England it could never have been once mentioned on the boat.'

In other words, Jardine did not bother talking about his leg-theory idea because it was still only a contingency plan he had roughed out in his mind, which he would try out if the right circumstances arose. He had satisfied himself that Larwood and Voce could bowl his leg-theory if called upon to do so, so there was no necessity to involve other members of the team in the plan until it had to be given a trial. Jardine was autocratic enough to feel no need to confer with his players. There was also a security consideration: Jardine would have realized that the fewer the people who knew about the idea, the less the chance of its becoming known to the Australians. Still, it must be considered extraordinary that Jardine did not let his vice-captain, Bob Wyatt, know what he had in mind. In *The Story of Warwickshire Cricket*, Wyatt is quoted as expressing the belief that an innings he played with a broken hand in 1931 convinced Jardine he 'was just the type for the dour struggle ahead in Australia'. But Wyatt was not made of nearly such stern stuff as Jardine, and, moreover, he was an amateur with strong loyalties to the game's traditions. Jardine may have sensed that Wyatt would not approve of his leg-theory (in the event, Wyatt did not approve of it) and he may have delayed confiding in him for that reason.

Arthur Mailey sailed to Australia on the *Orontes* with the English team, and he later recalled, 'During the voyage the members of the team danced, joined parties and played deck sports whilst their skipper sat in a quiet corner and read Chaucer.' Jardine had a great deal on his mind. Before the *Orontes* left Sri Lanka on the last leg of its voyage to Fremantle, he sent ahead a message of goodwill to Australians. 'I hope that the visit of the present team will create as much interest and good feeling as has been the case with past sides,' he said. 'Both England and Australia have been passing through difficult times in a manner worthy of our race . . . May the friendly rivalry of cricket, our joint national pastime, add its quota of cement to the foundations laid in the past.'

5
The Trap is Sprung

Don Bradman began the 1932–33 season in devastating form. In his first grade match at the beginning of October he made 108 for St George against Gordon, reaching his century in only sixty-four minutes. In his second grade match, against Mosman, he made 105 not out, and in the first of the NSW State trials he made 145 in 105 minutes, hitting 23 fours and two sixes. One of the opposing bowlers in this match, incidentally, was Alan McGilvray, the cricket broadcaster. Three days later, on 18 October, Jardine and his men arrived at Fremantle, and a few days after that Bradman began the long train journey to Perth to play for a Combined Australian XI against the Englishmen. Jack Fingleton, who travelled with him, said a prince could not have made a more regal entry to Perth. Thousands crowded the railway station and the streets outside to catch a glimpse of Bradman, making it necessary for the police to force a passage for him. Bradman's first encounter with the Englishmen was inconclusive. Larwood and Voce did not play, and Bradman made only 3 and 10 on a rain-affected wicket. There was a belief in the English camp that Bradman had been ill at ease against the bowling of Allen, who bowled very fast that day, but Bradman was hardly at the crease long enough for anyone to tell. However, Bradman did have one unexpected success: Jardine was caught by Stan McCabe off his bowling only two runs short of a century.

Bradman's failures against Jardine's team were a

tremendous disappointment for the 20,000 people who came along to see him bat, then a record attendance for the Perth ground, but, given the state of the wicket, not much importance was attached to them. In any case, Bradman demonstrated only a week later that he was playing as well as ever. In a Sheffield Shield match between NSW and Victoria, he scored 238 runs in 200 minutes, 128 of them in boundaries. In doing so he destroyed one of the strongest bowling attacks in Australian cricket, consisting of Harry Alexander, Don Blackie, L. O'B. Fleetwood-Smith and Bert Iron-monger, all of whom played Test cricket at one time or another. By now the Australian public had become accustomed to Bradman's high-speed double-centuries, but this innings was reckoned to be exceptional even for him, so complete was his mastery of the bowling. One cricket writer was prepared to say it was 'possibly his greatest innings in this country'. For the English-men, the Bradman threat loomed as large as ever.

For a time attention was focused on Bradman for another reason. Early in 1932 he had signed a three-way employment contract with the retailer F. J. Palmer, the radio station 2 UE, and the Sydney news-paper the *Sun*. At the time, the contract was hailed by many people, including several members of the Board of Control, as a guarantee that Bradman would not accept an offer from any of the Lancashire League clubs, one of which had recently been seeking his services. The contract was extremely important to Bradman. In 1932, remember, Australia was in the grip of the Depression, and the contract provided him with his only income. Moreover, in April that year he married Jessie Menzies, a friend from childhood, so his need for security was suddenly more pressing than ever.

Before the start of the 1932–33 season, however, the Board, which forbade its players to write for newspapers unless they were professional journalists, refused Bradman permission to write for the *Sun*, its reason being that journalism was not Bradman's sole means of livelihood. Bradman said he intended honouring the contract, even if it meant he would not play for Australia, but in the end the *Sun* released Bradman from his obligation to write for it, although it continued to pay him. It was an acrimonious affair, and it has considerable relevance to the bodyline story because of the mental strain it imposed on Bradman in the opening weeks of a season which promised to be stressful enough for other reasons. It may be noted, too, that Bradman had only recently returned from an unofficial tour of North America led by Arthur Mailey, during which he scored 4,000 runs in three months. He arrived back in Australia exhausted, to face the task of beginning married life, the row with the Board and the onslaught of England's fast bowlers. It was a trying time, indeed, for a man barely twenty-four years old.

Meanwhile, the tour by Jardine's men was proceeding uneventfully. They played two matches in Perth, against Western Australia and the Combined XI, and in both matches their bowling tactics were strictly conventional. There were a couple of incidents in Perth, however, which illustrated the seriousness of Jardine's purpose. Claude Corbett of the Sydney *Sun*, one of Australia's best-known sports writers at the time, suggested to Jardine that he release his team lists in the morning rather than the evening to enable afternoon newspapers such as his own to publish them first. According to Arthur Mailey, who was there, Jardine stiffened, frowned at Corbett and, after a long pause, said, 'What damned rot. We didn't come here to provide scoops for yours or any bally paper.' Corbett promptly sent off a story saying that the English captain was unco-operative and rude, and Mailey, to avoid further unpleasantness, arranged a meeting between Corbett and Jardine in Jardine's bedroom, at which the two agreed to forget the incident. But Jardine's relations with Australian journalists in general, and with Corbett in particular, remained bad throughout the tour. Tom Goodman, who covered the cricket that summer for the *Sydney Morning Herald*, recalls that any Australian journalist who approached Jardine could count on a frosty reception.

From Perth the English team travelled by train to Adelaide for the match against South Australia. Jardine made a reasonably brisk century in this match but was subjected to the same kind of barracking he had experienced in 1928–29, as a result of which Pelham Warner was moved to make the following remarks at a team reception:

'I have no axe to grind. It is many years since I was here, and the barracker was very good to me. If I have something to say now it is only because I have at heart the improvement of cricket, which I love and adore . . . We have to set an example, and now I am going to ask you a question. Do you think that it is quite dignified that the greatest cricket match in the world between the two greatest cricketing powers should be interrupted by a certain amount of noise?'

At this stage of the tour, Warner could still afford to be concerned with the game's niceties.

During the match at Adelaide, Jardine finally revealed his leg-theory plan to another of his fast bowlers, Bill Bowes. The tall, bespectacled Yorkshire-man had been bouncing the ball short at the South Australian batsmen, although with little effect, and

Jardine suggested to him, in a manner so obscure that Bowes had no idea what he was talking about, that he ought to bowl to a leg-theory field. Bowes recalls:

'Vic Richardson was batting – he pulled the ball very well, you know – and I bowled a bouncer and Vic pulled it, so I asked for a man over. Jardine said, "You can't have one." So I bowled another bouncer which Vic Richardson pulled, but I still didn't have a man over. So I bowled another bouncer again – this went on and I asked again for a man over. Jardine said, "No, but you can have three." I said, "Why three?" He had no reply: he walked away. So I bowled short until I was taken off. Jardine said afterwards, "I want to have a word with you." I said, "Yes, and I want to have a word with you, Skipper." Then, going back to the hotel he said, "Look, if you don't do as I tell you I'll send you home." So I said, "I'll go. I'll go tomorrow if you say so." He said, "Do you mean that?" I said, "Yes. I can't bowl just as you say if you don't tell me what your ideas are." And then he said he had this idea for leg-theory. It was the first time I'd heard about it.'

It may be concluded from all this that Jardine had not intended to show his hand at Adelaide, and that he suggested the leg-theory field to Bowes more or less on the spur of the moment. Otherwise, it might be asked, why would he have made the suggestion so abstrusely? The fact that he made the suggestion at all, though, indicates that the leg-theory idea was moving to the fore of his thinking. After Adelaide, the Englishmen moved on to Melbourne, and here at last the trap was sprung. The MCC played Victoria, and Voce bowled aggressively to a field which included three short-legs and a man behind them in the deep. Although Larwood did not play, Jack Fingleton regarded this match against Victoria as the one in which bodyline was used for the first time, even if in a modified form. Others, including Sir Donald Bradman, would argue that Voce's leg-theory bowling against Victoria did not constitute bodyline and that bodyline proper was not used until the next match, against an Australian XI, which began at the Melbourne Cricket Ground on 18 November. Larwood, too, believed this was so. 'We saved it up for the fifth match of the tour,' he said, 'because we wanted to get Don in strong company before giving him the full blast of our fast leg-theory tactic.'

Bradman played in this match, and so did all four of the English fast bowlers. Attracted by the prospect of seeing Bradman avenge himself for his failures in Perth, a crowd of 53,916 turned up on the Saturday, a world-record attendance at any match other than a Test. Larwood bowled very fast and repeatedly pitched the ball short, once hitting the opener Bill Woodfull in the chest with such force that for a moment it seemed he would collapse. Several of the English fieldsmen moved in to support him, but Woodfull recovered and resumed his innings a few minutes later. Thus, by the time Bradman came to the crease at the fall of the first wicket he knew exactly what he was up against, and from the outset it was clear he intended to meet violence with violence. He attacked Bowes at once and took 13 runs off a single over, but then Larwood was brought on at Bowes' end. It was the first time Bradman had faced Larwood that season, and, according to newspaper reports next day, the significance of the encounter was not lost on the huge crowd, which, we are told, 'confidently awaited the outcome of the duel'. Larwood's first ball to Bradman was short, and Bradman stepped back and crashed it to the point boundary, producing 'shrieks of delight' around the ground. The second ball was a full-blooded bouncer, which Bradman chose to duck. The next ball was also short, but Bradman hooked it over his shoulder in spectacular fashion for another four.

Then an ominous development: all but one of the slips fieldsmen moved across to take up positions on the leg-side. With the leg trap in place, Larwood made the ball fly viciously at Bradman on the line of the leg stump. A few overs later Bradman was given out lbw to Larwood when he tried to turn a ball to the on-side. Bradman did not query the decision, but many felt the umpire had erred, and erred badly. Bradman had made 36 in only forty-five minutes. It was an exciting, audacious innings, but Bradman never looked in command. In the second innings, he was bowled by Larwood for 13, but again he could consider himself unlucky. The light was bad, and the ball which bowled him barely rose above shin height. Still, it was his fourth failure in four innings against the Englishmen, some of whom began to sense a turning of the tables. Larwood was jubilant. Suddenly, he felt it was within his power to revenge himself for the indignities Bradman had made him suffer in 1930, and no bowler is more vengeful than a very fast bowler. 'I knew I had Don on the run,' Larwood wrote. 'I had upset his equilibrium and put him right off his game. Leg-theory had succeeded far better than I expected . . . I knew I had Don rattled.'

If the majority opinion of the matter can be accepted, bodyline proper was first bowled against Bradman and the other Australian XI batsmen on 19 November, only twelve days after Jardine made his clumsy disclosure of his leg-theory plans to Bill Bowes. What had happened in the meantime? Since the Englishmen began their tour at Perth, there had been a steady escalation in the use of leg-theory. In the two matches at Perth, there had been no leg-theory bowled at all. At Adelaide, leg-theory was not bowled, but Jardine did suggest its use to Bowes. In the first of the Melbourne matches, Voce bowled leg-theory and bowled it aggressively, but, Jack Fingleton's opinion notwithstanding, he seems to have stopped some distance short of bowling what came to be called bodyline. Finally, in the second of the Melbourne matches, we have Larwood bowling bodyline unadulterated and at full throttle. All this is consistent with the view held today by nearly all the survivors of Jardine's team that Jardine arrived in Australia with a rough idea which gradually evolved into bodyline. Allen, Wyatt, Ames, Bowes, even Larwood – they have all subscribed in print to the evolution theory. For instance, this is what Les Ames told Bill Evans of *Wisden Cricket Monthly* in December 1982:

'As far as I know it was never a planned exercise. I don't know how it started, and I'm not covering up for I don't think anyone else does. It may have been in Jardine's mind, but we certainly never had a meeting to discuss it. It just evolved.'

Yet the English fast bowlers turned on the heat so suddenly in Melbourne that it is difficult to believe they were not acting under instructions. They could not have done it, more or less spontaneously, of their own accord. It is easy to imagine Jardine taking Larwood, Voce and Bowes aside, perhaps on the train journey from Adelaide, and saying he wanted them to give the leg-theory plan he had been discussing with them a thorough try-out in Melbourne.

In fact, we would be entitled to believe such a meeting must have taken place if it were not for one strange circumstance. Jardine did not play in the Australian XI match; he was not there to see his strategy given its first trial against Bradman, the very man it was designed for. Instead, he spent the weekend trout-fishing, one of his favourite pastimes, at Tawonga on the Kiewa River near Albury. It was his deputy, Bob Wyatt, who marshalled England's bodyline forces for the first time, and Wyatt is adamant today that he did not follow any direction left behind by Jardine. He says his decision to move the fieldsmen into the leg-side cordon was a tactical one made in the course of the play, and its primary purpose was to stop the Australians scoring easy runs on the leg-side, not to intimidate them. 'It was quite obvious Bradman did not like the field placing. It worried him,' Wyatt says. 'When Jardine got back from his fishing trip I told him about it. He said, "Oh, that's interesting. We'll have to give him more of it."' According to Wyatt, the England selection committee afterwards discussed the possibilities of the leg-theory field placing, particularly in the light of the disconcerting effect it seemed to have on Bradman, and out of this, in his opinion, emerged bodyline. 'I am absolutely certain the whole thing gradually evolved,' he says. 'I think it evolved from that (Melbourne) field setting.'

Anyone seeking to trace the development of Jardine's bodyline concept might almost wish Bob Wyatt had kept this recollection to himself, for it introduces tremendous confusion in what might otherwise seem a fairly logical progression. Indeed, almost everything about that first trial of bodyline is confusing. Why did Jardine go off fishing? It is true he was due for a rest. At this stage of the tour he and Pataudi were the only members of the MCC team who had played in every match. Yet the match against the Australian XI was of immense importance to him personally as well as to his team. For the first time his entire battery of fast bowlers, on whom England's chances in the series clearly depended, was to be tested against Don Bradman. Let us assume for the moment, too, that Jardine knew Larwood would be trying out his leg-theory plan against Bradman. Under these circumstances, he should not have been able to take his eyes off the play for a moment. Lex Marinos, who helped write and direct the Kennedy-Miller television drama, *Bodyline*, found Jardine's absence from the Melbourne Cricket Ground that weekend the most baffling feature of the entire bodyline story, and he concluded there could have been only one explanation for it: Jardine was so keyed-up, so anxious, about the first trial of his leg-theory that he could not bear to watch it. This may seem at first out of character for a man of Jardine's mettle, but it does have an echo in Jardine's behaviour elsewhere. According to Bob Wyatt, Jardine hated the suspense of waiting to go in to bat; he was, he says, a 'bundle of nerves'. When Wyatt, an opener, was dismissed in the first Test in Sydney, he returned to the dressing room to find Jardine sitting behind a post where he could not see the play. 'I sat down next to him,' Wyatt says. 'I said, "A beautiful wicket – we'll make 500." He said, "You must be bloody crazy." He was so worked up that he'd got himself into a state.' It was because of his nervousness that the England selection committee decided he should open the batting, which he did for the last three Tests, to spare him the anxiety of sitting with his pads on. A man who could not bear to watch the play while awaiting his turn to bat might not have been able to watch, either, when the moment of truth arrived for his leg-theory brainchild.

This, however, does not help us fit Wyatt's leg-theory initiative into the picture. It cannot have been purely by coincidence that the tactics he used against

Bradman in Melbourne were virtually identical to the tactics Jardine had been preparing for Bradman since July. No, Jardine and his fast bowlers must have had some understanding about the tactics to be used in Melbourne. Larwood implied this when he wrote, 'We saved it up for the fifth match of the tour . . .' It must be remembered, too, that Jardine was in charge when Voce bowled leg-theory in the first match in Melbourne, against Victoria, the first occasion on which leg-theory of any kind had been bowled by the Englishmen that summer. To reconcile all this with Wyatt's account, we must conclude that the leg-side field was not set solely at Wyatt's instigation, but at the bowler's instigation, too.

Jardine must have been tremendously encouraged by what happened in the Australian XI match. In his book about the tour, *In Quest of the Ashes*, he said he had not been too optimistic about leg-theory's chances of success in 1932–33. 'I had never imagined that leg theory would stand such a test as would prove its effectiveness throughout the whole tour, but I did hope that it might occasionally prove a profitable variation when two batsmen were well set.' Jardine probably held higher hopes for leg-theory than he was prepared to admit here, yet he could not possibly have expected it to be as successful as it became. What he could not have foreseen when he roughed out his leg-theory plan in England was the fearsome pace Larwood would generate in Australia.

Larwood turned twenty-eight as the tour got under way, an age at which most fast bowlers have ceased to improve and are happy enough to maintain the speed they once had. Moreover, Larwood's mediocre performances against the Australians in 1928–29 and in

1930, when Bradman in particular gave him a pounding, could not have inspired Jardine with much confidence. Larwood himself was actually pessimistic about his chances of being chosen for the tour. Imagine Jardine's joy then at discovering Larwood was a faster and altogether better bowler in Australia than he had ever been. His speed was now terrific. Bert Oldfield, who had his skull fractured by Larwood later in the season, wrote:

> 'Not only did he increase his pace from that of four years earlier on his previous tour to express speed, but he showed the remarkable faculty for a fast bowler of being able to control to an uncanny extent his direction and length . . . I would say he was the fastest and most accurate bowler I have ever played against.'

Bradman, too, rated Larwood the fastest bowler he knew over a full season. 'At times he attained exceptional speed,' Bradman said. Larwood's own explanation for his extra speed in 1932–33 is that he was fitter than he had been before and he was able to gain a better foothold. In fact, it is probable that Larwood simply 'peaked' later than is usual for fast bowlers. For Jardine's purposes, he could not have peaked at a better time. After the Australian XI match, the *Daily Express* in London commented, 'Bradman did injurious things to Larwood's bowling analysis when the Australians were here. Now Larwood has begun to get his own back. We are witnessing not only a struggle between two teams, but a battle between two champions.'

There was but one more match to play before the first Test – against New South Wales in Sydney. Larwood was rested for this match, but Voce bowled bodyline of a most virulent kind. Voce was not exceptionally fast, but bowling left-arm around the wicket, he had the ability to make the ball kick nastily into the right-handed batsman. In both innings he bowled to a four-man leg trap covered by two other fieldsmen in the deep, generally pitching short on or outside the leg stump.

This match may be considered Jack Fingleton's match. He opened the batting for NSW in the first innings, carried his bat and made 119. Then twenty-four years old, Fingleton had made his Test debut against the South Africans in the previous season, and he was fighting now for a place in the Test side to play the Englishmen. His success in the NSW match was therefore opportune, but Fingleton later maintained that he derived no pleasure from it. During his long innings he was hit frequently on the body by Voce, but this first experience of bodyline made a deeper impression on him mentally than physically. In one of the most evocative passages in his book, *Cricket Crisis*, Fingleton wrote of his feelings at the end of the innings.

'I should have been deliriously happy as I returned to the pavilion, for was this not a complete realisation of a youthful dream? Could one have wished for a better answer to one's prayers, with Test selection against England also in the offing? There was, on the contrary, no wild thrill about it. I was conscious of a hurt, and it was not because of the physical pummelling I had taken from Voce. It was the consciousness of a crashed ideal. Playing against England in actuality had proved vastly different from what boyish dreams and adventure had imagined it to be. The game was not the thing, but also seemed to be the last thing.'

The veteran journalist R. W. E. Wilmot supplied an interesting note on Voce's bowling against NSW. He said that at the end of the match he examined the wicket carefully and found 'unmistakable evidence' that many of Voce's deliveries had pitched within 24 feet, or 7.3 metres, of the bowling crease.

Bradman played for NSW and failed in both innings, scoring only 18 and 23. In the second innings he stepped inside a short-pitched ball from Voce, apparently in expectation of its being a bouncer, but the ball did not rise and Bradman had his middle stump knocked over behind his back. It was an inglorious way to be dismissed, but Bradman had spent the previous day ill in bed and, in fact, won praise from the press just for appearing at the crease, so some allowance had to be made for that. Still, he had now made only 103 runs in six innings against the Englishmen, which seemed to indicate a trend. In England, though, the commentators viewing events from afar hardly dared to hope that the English fast bowlers really had Bradman's measure. The theme of comments in the London press was that Bradman was merely going through a bad patch, from which he was sure to emerge soon. But one noted cricket writer, William Pollock of the *Daily Express*, did mention the previously unthinkable – dropping Bradman from the Australian team. 'He is not worth a place on his present form,' Pollock said. 'It is no secret that the leg-theory bowling of Larwood and Voce rattles him.' Yet Pollock, too, admitted that Bradman was liable to score a double-century at any time. The London-based Australian actor Oscar Asche, a cricket enthusiast, was inspired to write a poem in defence of Bradman, which concluded with the lines:

> *Come, Bradman, rise, strike out, belittlers stun;*
> *By fresh deeds prove you are still Don – not done.*

On 30 November, Jardine made a breezy speech at a city luncheon, but his parting words had a dire ring to them. 'If we offend anyone in this country, then I would ask you to be very charitable, because I am quite certain that it is not intentional.' The first Test was due to start two days later.

6
McCabe's Finest Hour

On the eve of the first Test in Sydney, it was announced that Don Bradman was unfit and would not play. This was a cause of bitter disappointment, not merely for those Sydney people who had been looking forward to seeing him play, but for cricket followers throughout the country, to whom a Test match without Bradman hardly seemed a Test match at all. Bradman's ailment was never specified. The two doctors who examined him told the Board of Control that he was organically sound but in a seriously run-down condition. He also had a sore throat, which seems to have been associated with the complaint that kept him in bed for a day earlier that week during the MCC's match against NSW. In his autobiography, Bradman said that 'the strain of cricket and travel and argument was beginning to tell' and had affected his batting in the MCC–NSW match. The 'argument' Bradman refers to here was almost certainly the one he had with the Board of Control at the start of the season over his contract to write for a newspaper.

All this seems to indicate that Bradman was suffering from nervous exhaustion, a condition not uncommon in people subjected to intense and constant pressure. Jardine believed Bradman had had a nervous break-down. He said so in a book he wrote a few years later, *Ashes – and Dust*. For nearly three years Bradman had been subjected to publicity more intense than any Australian had known before, or probably has since.

The Australian nation was preoccupied by him. William Pollock, who visited Australia in the 1930s, wrote, 'Australia is Bradman mad. You hear his name all day long in the mouths of men, women and children – in the cricket season. Everything he says or does – or is supposed to say or do – is seized upon.'

Bradman was admired on all sides for keeping a level head while all this attention was being focused on him, but it must have worn away at his nerves. On top of that there was the pressure of having constantly to meet the public's expectations of him. Bradman would have experienced this in every match he played: the crowds came not only to see him bat, they came to see him score a century. In match after match he was expected to perform like a superman. When he played in a Test, he carried the hopes of a whole nation. Only someone possessing great mental discipline could have coped with this kind of pressure, and throughout his long career Bradman seems to have coped with it amazingly well. Yet in 1932–33 he had a special problem: millions of Australians looked to him to overcome the shock tactics, as they were called, of the English fast bowlers, but by this time Bradman may already have come to believe that bodyline could not be mastered. He certainly came to that conclusion later. We know Bradman was very conscious of the fact that the Australian public was counting on him not just to withstand the English fast bowlers but to triumph over them. A. G. Moyes, who was consulted by Bradman at the time, wrote that the public's expectation of him was one of Bradman's chief considerations when he was trying to devise a counter strategy. This, then, may well have been Bradman's difficulty: the Australian public was confident he could accomplish what he himself guessed was beyond his powers. If he was under nervous strain because of it, we should not be too surprised.

With Bradman absent, the first Test began as something of an anti-climax, yet by stumps on the first day, and certainly by lunchtime on the second, it had come to be considered one of the great occasions in the game's history. Australia batted first, and against an extremely hostile bodyline attack Stan McCabe batted as a man inspired, scoring 187 not out in just over four hours. During those four hours bodyline looked to be a failed enterprise. Voce, whose stock ball seemed to be the bouncer, and Larwood, who again bowled very fast, both took a pasting. Bill O'Reilly, who played in this match, has always held that if Bradman had been fit enough to play and had been in with McCabe, attacking the bowling at the other end, bodyline might have been discarded by Jardine there and then as an unsuccessful experiment.

Stan McCabe was then twenty-two years old, a likeable, easy-going country boy who did not take himself or even his cricket too seriously. He was shortish (5' 8" or 173 cm) and still in possession of a youthfully trim figure, which was destined before too long to become well-rounded. To listen to contemporaries such as Gubby Allen speak of him today is to realize that he was considered by them not to be just another very good Test batsman, but a batsman of absolutely the highest class. Allen thinks McCabe's performances never did his great ability justice. He believes he would have been a more successful batsman if there had been no Bradman, his reasoning being that the presence of such a prodigious scorer higher up the batting list dulled McCabe's incentive to make big scores himself. McCabe was, incidentally, the only Australian batsman who scored faster than Bradman in the Tests in 1930. Bradman, as we have seen, scored at the rate of 3.7 runs for each six balls faced. McCabe scored at the rate of 4.1 runs for each six balls faced. McCabe's parents had come down from his home town, Grenfell, to see their son play in the Sydney Test, and he sat with them until it was his turn to pad up. Before he left he said to his father, 'If I happen to get hit out there, keep Mum from jumping the fence.'

It is Harold Larwood's opinion that McCabe played the hook shot as brilliantly as Bradman, but he did not have Bradman's gift of keeping the ball down when he played it. A. G. Moyes cited McCabe's tendency to hook in the air as one of the flaws in his technique. Theoretically, therefore, bodyline should have made short work of him, for McCabe played the hook shot and the pull shot in this innings with abandon. A diagram prepared by the scorers showed that of McCabe's twenty-five boundary strokes fifteen were played between backward square leg and mid-wicket. The other boundaries were scored mainly by cuts and glances, and only one was scored by a drive – through the covers off Voce. That he did not get caught by one of the leg-side fieldsmen seems to have been largely a matter of luck. The ball simply did not go to hand. McCabe freely admitted later that he owed much of his success to luck. His innings was a '"Sydney-or-the-bush" gamble,' he said. 'I had a charmed life. I was lucky. I could have been out any time.' He was not blessed by luck again. In the other nine innings he played in the Tests that summer, he scored only 198 runs. For the time being, however, he was a national hero, although this did not turn his head by one degree. McCabe told the Test selector E. A. Dwyer afterwards that he had refrained from reading the newspaper accounts of his innings. 'I took a book to read on the ferry,' McCabe said. 'I thought there might be a lot of exaggerated praise in them (the newspapers) that it wouldn't do me any good to read.'

Australia made 360 in its first innings, but England easily surpassed this with 524. Three Englishmen scored centuries – Sutcliffe 194, Hammond 112 and the Nawab of Pataudi 102. The Australians had half-hoped that a tall Victorian pace bowler named Lisle Nagel, playing in his first Test, might work wonders for them, but no wonders were forthcoming. Nagel, 6' 6″ (198 cm) played for the Australian XI in Melbourne and took eight English wickets for only 32 runs. This feat earned him a place in the Test side, but he took only two wickets for 110 runs, and those were the wickets of men who had passed the century, Hammond and Pataudi. Nagel never played in a Test again. In the second innings, Australia succumbed to Larwood's pace and fire, and was all out for 164. England thus needed to score only one run to win the match, which it did by ten wickets.

Amid all the excitement over McCabe's innings, it might easily have been overlooked that Larwood and Voce bowled bodyline in this match more vigorously than ever before. It was double-barrelled bodyline, bowled at both ends by Larwood and Voce in alternation, apparently for the first time on the tour. Voce bowled more bouncers than Larwood and as a result was barracked more by the crowd, but Larwood's bodyline was the more fearsome, and by far the more effective, of the two. Pelham Warner said in *Cricket Between Two Wars* that in one period 39 of 42 deliveries by Larwood in this match were directed on or near the line of the batsman. The important thing was that Larwood took five wickets in each innings and was largely responsible for England's comfortable win.

Despite the four-hour setback it received from McCabe, bodyline had proved to be a huge success. This was not just because of the occasional catches the Australian batsmen cocked up to the fieldsmen in the leg trap, as Fingleton did in the first innings when he tried to fend off a rising ball from Larwood. Even more important was the debilitating effect it had on the Australian batsmen generally; they were unsettled by it, and it showed in the way they played. Bill Ponsford, the man reputed to have the broadest bat in the world, was twice bowled behind his legs, first by Larwood and then, in the second innings, by Voce, just as Bradman had been in the MCC–NSW match. As a result, Ponsford would be left out of the Australian eleven in the second Test.

Bodyline's saddest casualty of all in the first Test was Alan Kippax. This tall, elegant, thoughtful, gentlemanly player found bodyline more than he could handle, or wished to handle, at the age of thirty-five. Kippax was then one of the most distinguished of all Australian cricketers. He had come to the fore in the 1920s, a batsman whose natural grace reminded older men of Victor Trumper, and as recently as 1930 he had averaged 54.8 in a Test series against England. But in the previous season, 1931–32, he had twice been hit on the head, first in a country match at Parkes and then in a match against Queensland in Brisbane. He was in no fit state of mind, therefore, to face up to the barrage from Larwood and Voce. Larwood dismissed him in both innings, for 8 and 19. After he was out in the first innings, he is said to have confessed to his team-mates, 'He's too bloody fast for me.' In 1981 Bill Voce told Murray Hedgcock in an interview for *Wisden Cricket Monthly*, 'Bradman didn't like bodyline, but he didn't show it in the way some of them did. Kippax was scared stiff, and he let you see it.'

Kippax was dropped from the side after the first Test and was not reinstated. The sad irony is that in his prime he was a marvellous hooker of fast bowling, and in 1928–29 he gave Larwood some rough treatment.

Among the spectators at the first Test was a veteran of the very first Test played between Australia and England in 1877, Tom Garrett. Up to this point, the Australian journalists covering the tour had criticized Jardine's tactics in only the mildest terms, but Garrett, then seventy-four years old, was so affronted by them that he went into print at once himself by writing letters to the *Sydney Morning Herald*. In the first of them, which appeared on the day after the Test ended, he said:

'I played cricket for many years in Australia, and also in England, and against the fastest bowlers of my time, Tom Richardson, Ernie Jones, Crossland and others, and I can unhesitatingly say that this is the first occasion that I have seen bowlers deliberately bowling at the batsman. If this system of bowling is persevered with, then all the beautiful cricket strokes played by the English and Australian batsmen in the past will be eliminated from the game, which in a few years' time will be either played by youths only or will come to resemble baseball in its padding and protection to players.'

The debate about Jardine's methods was only really beginning, and for the moment Jardine showed some readiness to enter it. From Sydney the MCC team travelled to Tasmania, and on their arrival in Launceston on 15 December Jardine made the following statement defending his leg-theory:

'Any team has a right to play any theory so long as it does not infringe the rules of cricket. The leg-theory tactics of the Englishmen are equally open to the Australian bowlers to emulate. These can be overcome, and this has been proved by the way McCabe, Cummins [F. S. Cummins, who batted at number seven for NSW against the MCC and scored 71 in 77 minutes] and Fingleton handled this type of bowling. The leg-theory seems to have had its birth in Australian newspapers. We knew nothing about it, but we have read about it since. Exactly the same type of attack has been tried times without number, from Test cricket to village cricket. Where we have been successful has been in the playing of the leg field, and up to date these tactics have been rather disastrous to batsmen. The practice is nothing new, and there is nothing dangerous about it. I hope it goes on being successful.'

Here we have the lines already drawn for the war of words about bodyline which was soon to be waged. Garrett, who has been watching Test cricket since 1877, says he has just witnessed something radically new – bowlers deliberately bowling at the batsmen. Jardine says the Englishmen's methods have been used often before, in all kinds of cricket. This was the principal point of contention about bodyline in the months that followed and, to some extent, it is still a point of contention, more than fifty years later. By now Jardine had begun to receive hate mail. One Tasmanian man warned him in a letter that he intended writing to King George V to inform him about the unfair tactics Jardine was using. For some reason Jardine went to the trouble of sending the man a reply on 17 December, a copy of which somehow found its way into the Australian Cricket Board's archives. Jardine's note at least contained a streak of humour. 'What fun you must have counting people out on the wireless and writing to HM the King,' he said. 'Here's wishing you a Merry Christmas and lots more fun in the New Year.' It seems Jardine did have a sense of humour, even if he did not reveal it to everyone. John Arlott, who got to know him well after the war, says,

'He was a witty man with a terribly dry sense of humour. He was very funny – he could paralyse you with laughter.'

It was during the first Test, by all accounts, that the word 'bodyline' was coined. The generally accepted version of the story is that in cabling a match report to his newspapers from the Sydney Cricket Ground a journalist condensed the phrase 'on the line of the body' to 'bodyline', which because of its succinctness caught on at once. That journalist was widely held to have been Hugh Buggy, then of the Melbourne *Herald*, who was possibly Australia's best-known newspaper-man between the wars. Larwood, in his book, said Jardine blamed Buggy for creating the term and bore him something of a grudge because of it. Yet doubt about the origin of the word persists. Jack Fingleton thought Buggy was responsible for it but clearly was not sure, and Fingleton was a man of an inquiring mind who would certainly have done his best to find out. The word was not a neutral one: there was a condemnation of Jardine's tactics implicit in it, which is the reason the Englishmen took exception to it and refused to recognize it. There are members of Jardine's side, some of them opponents of bodyline at the time, who after all these years can hardly bring themselves to use it. Because the word 'bodyline' was new, it reinforced the idea in Australian minds that bodyline itself was new, and not the same as the leg-theory which had been bowled for generations. That was its wider importance.

7

Bradman's Triumph

It is a mistake to think that bodyline caused widespread outrage in Australia as soon as it was bowled. The truth is that the newspapers, still the chief source of information about the game for most Australians, were slow to condemn it, and in some cases even slow to describe it, and as a result public opinion was slow to turn against it, too. There were several reasons why this was so. In the first place, cricket writers did not recognize immediately the nature of the Englishmen's tactics. In their reports of the earlier matches there was frequent reference to the Englishmen's short-pitched bowling but often no reference at all to the cordon of short-leg fieldsmen, although we can tell from other sources that such a field was set. The men in the press box did not perceive at once the crucial interrelation between the two. Moreover, some Australian newspapers, perhaps most of them, did not find it easy to accuse a team of English cricketers of unsportsmanlike conduct. To do so seemed almost disloyal.

Tom Goodman, who covered the series for the *Sydney Morning Herald*, is interesting on this point. He says some editors could not bring themselves to believe that an Englishman of Jardine's background would do anything unfair, and initially they were reluctant to publish stories which suggested it. The *Sydney Morning Herald* went so far as to publish an editorial on the last day of the first Test defending Jardine's tactics. 'It is puerile to complain of the

Englishmen's "shock bowling" as something unfair,'
the *Herald* said. '. . . As for the bumping ball, have
Australians no memory? Are Jones, Cotter, McDonald
and Gregory so soon forgotten? Did they never make
the ball fly high at the batsman here and in England?'
Six weeks later, after Bert Oldfield had his skull
fractured, the *Herald* published an editorial condemning the same kind of bowling.

There is one other factor to consider here, and it
is one which Sir Donald Bradman himself views as
important. In each of the first four matches in which
bodyline was bowled, there was excitement of some
other kind to distract the attention of the crowds, the
cricket writers and the public at large from the tactics of
the English fast bowlers. In the first of these matches,
against the Australian XI in Melbourne, it was the
sensational bowling performance by Lisle Nagel, who,
remember, took 8 for 32, not Larwood's bodyline
bowling, which made the biggest headlines. In the
second match, against NSW, Larwood did not play,
and in any case Jack Fingleton scored a gallant century,
which effectively pushed Voce's bodyline bowling into
the background. It was the same in the first Test –
Australians were too excited about McCabe's marvellous innings to worry much about the ethics of the
English bowling. The fourth match in which bodyline
was used was the second Test. Bradman made a
century, Bill O'Reilly took ten wickets and Australia
won a most satisfying victory. Again, Australians could
afford to overlook Jardine's tactics.

Bradman watched the Test in Sydney, for part of
the time from the Australian dressing room, and then
had a short holiday on the south coast of New South
Wales, staying in a beach cottage owned by the NSW
cricket team's masseur, Tom Langridge. His reason

for going there was to rest and recover his health, but he was not entirely idle. He used the time to work out a method of dealing with Jardine's leg-theory. On the day after his return to Sydney he went to see A. G. 'Johnnie' Moyes, the sports editor of the *Sun* newspaper, who had taken a fatherly interest in Bradman since he first arrived from Bowral. Moyes was a former first-class cricketer with a deep knowledge of the game, and Bradman wanted him to find flaws in the counterstrategy he had devised. This is how Moyes described that strategy:

> 'He would walk away from his wicket and try to hit the ball through the off-side field. If he succeeded it would put the bowler off his balance and would force him to weaken the leg field and strengthen the off field. Then he could revert to normal batsmanship. His plan was, in effect, to meet unorthodoxy with unorthodoxy – he must make runs.'

Bradman had ruled out the pull shot because of the physical risk it entailed; Larwood moved the ball into the batsman, so a fractured skull was always a possibility if he failed to connect. He had also ruled out the hook shot, reasoning that a man of his height could not hope to get on top of the ball. It is faintly ironical that Jardine afterwards queried Bradman's decision to forsake the hook. Nobody played the stroke better than Bradman, Jardine said, and this made his comparative failure against Larwood in Australia appear all the more remarkable. Moyes does not seem to have queried it, though. He was more worried by the prospect of Bradman being bowled as he stepped away to cut by a ball which kept lower than he expected. Bradman's answer to this objection was that he would not pull away to cut unless the ball was genuinely short – that is, short enough to bounce over the stumps. The journalist R. W. E. Wilmot reported one other adjustment Bradman made to his technique: instead of taking guard on centre-and-leg as he had in the past, he took guard on the leg stump. The object here, probably, was to encourage bowlers who bowled at the batsman to pitch the ball further towards the leg-side, thereby reducing the chances of them bowling him with a ball that kept low.

Moyes found Bradman looking better and fit for action, if not completely well. There were other indications in the following fortnight that his health had improved. On 19 December he drove with his wife from Bowral to Melbourne in one day, completing the journey in fifteen hours. Bradman was said to have a talent for fast driving, and he must have motored along at a lively rate that day to cover the distance so quickly on the roads of 1932. Apart from all that, the trip showed Bradman had plenty of stamina. Then, on Boxing Day, he made 157 for NSW against Victoria in Melbourne. He batted cautiously until he reached his century, as if playing himself back into form, but made his last 50 in half an hour. The innings augured well for the second Test.

The second Test began on 30 December. The team which Jardine announced that morning indicated plainly enough what his intentions were. He and the other England selectors chose to play all four fast bowlers, Larwood, Voce, Allen and Bowes, and had dropped the only spinner, Verity. Even in the 1980s, a period which has seen a greater reliance on fast bowling in international cricket than ever before, an all-pace attack is still considered unusual and worthy of comment. In 1932 the presence of four fast bowlers in one side (the fifth bowler, Hammond, bowled medium pace) was considered outlandish. Jardine obviously intended keeping the Australians under constant pressure by having all four of his fast bowlers bowl bodyline in rotation. Of these four, only Gubby Allen was not by now a practised exponent of the new tactics. Up to this point Allen had not bowled bodyline at all, and Jardine had not asked him to bowl it, no doubt because he sensed Allen did not approve of it.

George Oswald Browning Allen had a background not unlike Jardine's. He was born at Rose Bay in Sydney in July 1902, and he came from a prominent family of lawyers. His great-grandfather, George Allen, started a law practice in Sydney in the early 1800s, and his grandfather, Sir George Allen, was a leading lawyer, businessman and politician. He was New South Wales Minister for Justice and Speaker of the Legislative Assembly. Gubby's father, Walter, took his family to England to live while Gubby was still a child, and Gubby was educated at Eton and Cambridge. Allen was a gentleman cricketer like Jardine. Indeed, it seems he was better off than Jardine and may well have been considered socially superior to him.

Allen was only one of a number of English players who objected on principle to bodyline bowling, but he was the only English fast bowler who objected to it, so he was faced with a special dilemma. He was prepared to go along with the bodyline plan to the extent of fielding in the bodyline trap (as we shall see, one other English player was not prepared on one occasion to go even this far), but he drew the line at bowling it. Allen was the second-fastest bowler Jardine had – Larwood thinks Allen actually bowled faster than he did in England in 1930 – and Jardine would have wanted him to bowl the new leg-theory if only for that reason. It is also likely, however, that Jardine wanted Allen, an ex-Eton amateur, to bowl it because of the respectability he would automatically have given it.

Before play on the first morning of the Melbourne Test, Jardine finally asked Allen to bowl the new leg-theory, and Allen refused. This is Allen's account of what was said:

> 'Douglas came to me in the dressing room and he said, "I want you to bowl a few more bouncers and have a stronger leg-side-field," or words to that effect. I said, "No, Douglas, I never bowl like that and I don't think it's the way the game should be played." He said, "You've got to do it," and I said, "Well, Douglas, I'm not going to and you'll have to make up your mind whether you want me to play or not." I left him, but later I said, "Am I playing?" and he said, "Of course you're playing. What are you talking about?" and away we went and I bowled just as I always have bowled. He never once tackled me again. To his great credit he accepted my point of view and we remained the best of friends throughout the tour.'

It hardly needs to be pointed out that Jardine did not take nearly as tough a line with Allen here as he did with Bill Bowes when Bowes was insubordinate in Adelaide. Jardine threatened to send Bowes back to England, but Bowes was a professional and Allen was an amateur, and even so resolute a leader as Jardine would have baulked at the idea of sending home an amateur. We are left to wonder what Jardine would have done if one of the professional fast bowlers, Larwood, Voce or Bowes, had refused on principle, as Allen did, to bowl bodyline.

Before he had this confrontation with Jardine in Melbourne, Allen had confided his views to Bob Wyatt, another dissenter from Jardine's policy. Allen recalls:

'We were just getting a little suspicious that things were building up and Bob and I discussed it. I said I was dead against any rough stuff and he said so was he. But we decided that while we might discuss it among ourselves we must never at any moment start talking to other members of the team about it and we should never discuss it with anybody in Australia at all. I never, never did.'

Bill Bowes remembers Allen's silent protest. 'When we had team discussions about tactics Gubby would just keep quiet,' he says. 'He didn't give any dissenting voice or anything, he just kept quiet.' Allen says he opposed Jardine on only one other occasion. 'One day when we were miles away from the cricket ground, I did say, "Oh, Douglas, please try and quieten it down a bit – it really is getting rather awful," and he didn't answer.'

We do not know how Jardine was affected personally by this opposition from his own players to what he was doing, but we may surmise it would have perturbed him more than the combined animosity of all 6.5 million Australians. It certainly weakened his position more than anything else, and it is as well for him that Allen, Wyatt and the other dissenters kept as quiet about their opposition to bodyline as they did. If the Australian press had learned of it – and it did catch a whisper of it once or twice – Jardine would have found it far more difficult to persevere with the bodyline attack and the MCC would have found it far more difficult to support him.

Australia made three changes to its team for the second Test – the veteran spinner Bert Ironmonger for Nagel, the young Victorian left-hander Leo O'Brien for Ponsford, and Bradman for Kippax. Australia batted first, and fielding near the boundary early in the innings Bob Wyatt heard some spectators shout at him, 'Wait till our Don comes in.' Bradman was the big attraction, and the attendance, 63,993, a world record for a cricket match, showed how big an attraction he was. When Bradman came in at 2.57 P.M. at the fall of the second wicket he was given an ovation which resounds in the memory of anyone who heard it. The applause rolled on and on like thunder until some time after Bradman had arrived at the crease. Then a momentous anti-climax. Bradman was bowled first ball. He swung mightily at a short delivery from Bowes outside the off stump and dragged it into the base of the leg stump. The crowd was shocked into silence. Bowes, too, was stunned. But Jardine, fielding at backward short-leg, reacted quickly and joyfully. He danced in a circle with his hands above his head – as Bowes says, rather like a Red Indian.

It may be argued that Bradman was a victim of Jardine's leg-theory no less than if he had been caught in the bodyline trap fending off a bouncer from Larwood. The daring and violence of the stroke indicated he was not in a normal frame of mind when he came to the wicket, and for that bodyline can probably be blamed. Bowes says that before he bowled that ball he knew as surely as if Bradman had told him himself that Bradman expected the ball to be a bouncer.

There was another happening on the field that day which some would say was of enormous significance, although nobody realized it at the time. Larwood tore his left boot while bowling and left the field to get another, but then he tore this second boot, too, and had to leave the field again. Altogether, he was off the field four times, once for twenty-two minutes, much to the annoyance of both Jardine and the crowd, which jeered at Larwood loudly. Larwood had to resort to wearing a brand new pair of boots which rubbed the

skin off his toes, and the pain, the jeering and Jardine's
lack of sympathy combined to make him very angry. 'I
was wild about the crowd's attitude,' Larwood said in
The Larwood Story. 'I bowled as hard as I could. The
harder I bowled the more it hurt, and the more it hurt
the harder I bowled.' It is Gubby Allen's belief that
bodyline proper came into being during this furious
spell of bowling by Larwood. Until then, he says, the
Englishmen had really been bowling only fast leg-
theory, admittedly of a most aggressive kind. This is
his account of how, in his opinion, the transition to
genuine bodyline came about:

> 'Harold busted his boots and was twice off the field for quite
> a little time. The crowd was yelling 'Put Larwood on,' and
> the atmosphere was getting pretty tense, not only in the
> crowd but amongst the players as well. Now back comes
> Harold and Douglas asked me to tell him to bowl – he
> wouldn't speak to him. Harold's temper was up a bit, and he
> rushed in and started to bowl a lot of bouncers. As he did
> bowl the bouncers, Douglas moved more fielders onto the
> leg-side and brought them up into closish positions. It was
> the first sign of what in my opinion became bodyline.'

It should be noted again, however, that it is the
general view of Australians who played in 1932–33 that
bodyline came into being at least three matches earlier.
Sir Donald Bradman, for instance, has no doubt that
what was bowled to him in the Austrlian XI match in
mid-November was bodyline, 'flat out and vicious'.

Australia made 228 and England could manage only
169 in reply. The wicket clearly suited the spin of the
Australians better than the speed of the Englishmen,
so if only Australia could make a reasonable fist of its
second innings it stood a good chance of levelling
the series. Again attention turned towards Bradman.

Bodyline

Knowing he was sure to bat, 68,188 people went to the
Melbourne Cricket Ground on Monday, an attendance
which broke the world record set on Friday, the first
day of the match. This time Bradman did not fail
them. Playing a steady rather than a brilliant innings,
he was 103 not out when the last Australian batsman
went out. There was a statistical peculiarity about this
score. It happened to be the same as the total of runs,
103, which Bradman had scored in the seven innings
he had played previously against the Englishmen that
season. It also restored his average in Tests against
England to precisely 103 – 1,545 runs in fifteen completed innings.

Bradman's triumph encouraged cricket writers to
declare that Jardine's leg-theory had been overcome.
Even Larwood was worried. 'He played well enough
to make me think he might yet tame bodyline . . . I
had my doubts about how I'd go in the following
Tests,' Larwood said. For the most part Bradman's
batting was orthodox in this innings. Larwood and
Voce were not so hostile on the sluggish Melbourne
wicket, and Bradman had little need to adopt the
unconventional methods he had discussed with Johnnie
Moyes. Vic Richardson, too, who twice scored in the
thirties in this match, handled the bowling with an
ease which should have raised Australian hopes that
bodyline could be mastered. In the second innings he
played Voce, in particular, so confidently that Voce
moved his fieldsmen back to the off-side and reverted
to orthodox bowling. In the second innings, only one
Australian batsman could have been counted a victim
of bodyline – Bill Woodfull, who popped a catch to
Allen at short-leg while playing defensively at a shortish ball from Larwood. On the other hand, the Melbourne wicket was easier-paced than the Australians

could hope to bat on again and, so far as we know, Jardine's confidence in his leg-theory did not waver.

Notwithstanding Bradman's century, Australia made only 191 in its second innings, setting England 251 to win. The openers, Sutcliffe and Leyland, took the score past 50 before the first wicket fell, but then there was a startling collapse, five wickets falling for 34 runs, followed by a brief rally and finally another collapse, as a result of which England was all out for 139. O'Reilly took five wickets, bringing his match total to ten, and Ironmonger took four. Afterwards, the respected critic E. P. Barbour pronounced O'Reilly the best spin bowler in the world, a ranking he retained throughout the 1930s.

It is said that during the second Test the Nawab of Pataudi told Jardine he did not wish to field in the bodyline cordon, prompting Jardine to remark, 'I see His Highness is a conscientious objector.' According to one version of the story, this happened after Woodfull was hit by Larwood. When Pataudi declined to move into the cordon, Jardine sent Verity there instead. It is not clear who first recorded this story, but Bill O'Reilly tells it with confidence, and O'Reilly was there. We do know that Pataudi had not objected previously to fielding in the bodyline cordon. In fact, he was fielding there with Jardine, Sutcliffe and Hammond when Bill Voce bowled the second over of the match. Perhaps he refused to return there because Woodfull had been hit or perhaps it was because, as Gubby Allen has reported, Larwood was bowling more bouncers than ever before. In any event, it could not have been easy for a young man of twenty-two, even an Indian prince of twenty-two, to defy someone as formidable as Jardine, and we are entitled to wonder whether there was not some special friction between

him and Jardine. In his book Larwood says plainly,
'Pataudi didn't like Jardine and made no secret of it,'
and he goes on to accuse Pataudi of leaking information
to Australian newspapers about dissension in the English team to embarrass Jardine.

After the second Test, Pataudi virtually bows out of
the bodyline story. He made a century in the first Test
but failed in the second, and was left out of the Test
side thereafter, some say because of his slow batting,
others because of his insubordination. Wyatt, a selector, said the selectors wanted to bring Eddie Paynter,
a left-hander, into the team to help counter O'Reilly,
and Pataudi was the one chosen to make way for him
because 'he had allowed the bowlers to dictate to him'.
And Wyatt had no personal axe to grind.

Pataudi had an unhappy tour. He was treated harshly
by the England selectors and harshly by the Australian
barrackers, who made him a butt for jokes such as
'Hey Gandhi – where's your goat?' and 'Hey Gandhi –
where's your loin cloth?' They also called him Pat
O'Day and Potato. Pataudi was sensitive enough,
proud enough, to be hurt by it. When he returned to
his home in India, in advance of the rest of the English
team, it must have been with relief.

8
Shocks at Adelaide

The extraordinary events which took place during the third Test at Adelaide and afterwards make a good deal more sense if they are viewed not in isolation but in relation to the summer-long campaign Jardine was waging to subdue Bradman and regain the Ashes. On the eve of the Adelaide Test it would have seemed to Jardine that, on the whole, his campaign had been extremely successful. Never had Bradman been dismissed so often so cheaply as he had by Jardine's bowlers that season. Who could have foreseen before the tour began that the Englishmen would get him out seven times for no more than 103 runs? It proved beyond doubt that fast leg-theory was effective against him, as Jardine had theorized months before that it might be. Tactically, it was quite an accomplishment. He had identified the enemy's 'weakness', devised a special plan to exploit it and then executed the plan with stunning success. He had achieved what most people would have considered all but impossible: reduced Don Bradman's scoring to mediocre proportions. So much the better that his leg-theory had proved equally as effective against every other leading Australian batsman.

But now his campaign had faltered. Bradman had made a century against his leg-theory bowlers and he might have made a double-century if the other Australian batsmen had been able to stay with him. Jardine would have noticed that Bradman's return to form had jolted the confidence of Harold Larwood.

Like Larwood, he was well aware of what Bradman was capable, and it would have seemed to him imperative to nip Bradman's revival in the bud lest it blossomed into double or even triple-centuries in the remaining Tests. The trouble in Melbourne had been that the leg-theory attack had been neither concentrated enough nor hostile enough. That was the fault of the pitch. In Adelaide, however, the pitch promised to be lively. Larwood and Voce had to get on top of Bradman again quickly in Adelaide, and the way to do that was to bowl their leg-theory more vigorously than ever before.

Thus, the tightening of the screws in Adelaide may be seen as Jardine's tactical response to the success of the Australians, and of Bradman in particular, in Melbourne. There is evidence that he had by now come to adopt a most combative attitude towards the Australians, possibly for the purpose of infusing a combative spirit into his men. Bob Wyatt recalls that Jardine used to say the Australian batsmen were 'yellow', meaning cowardly. When a new Australian batsman was on his way to the crease, Jardine would often make a derisive remark about him, such as 'Get ready . . . here comes another yellow bastard.' He certainly tried to psyche up his players in the dressing room, especially if they had to get Bradman out. Gubby Allen remembers Jardine saying 'some pretty rough things about Don to stir us up'. According to a third member of Jardine's team, if Bradman was in or about to come in Jardine would say to his men through clenched teeth, 'Come on – we've got to get the little bastard out.'

The Englishmen, having realized in Melbourne the folly of being without a spinner on a spinner's wicket, decided to take Verity into the Test instead of Bowes.

The Australians made only one change, Ponsford back in place of O'Brien. Jardine won the toss for the first and last time in the series, and chose to bat. England began badly, losing four wickets for 30, but Leyland and Wyatt dug in and between them raised the score to 186. Paynter, who came in then, scored 77, and eventually the total rose to a satisfactory 341. The England innings ended at 3.05 P.M. on the second day, Saturday, which meant Australia had little more than two hours' batting before stumps.

The attendance, 50,962, a record for the ground, testified to the intense public interest in the series. Adelaide's population at the time was 313,000, which means that a sixth of it was at the Adelaide Oval that day.

Australia began badly. Allen got Fingleton for a duck in his first over, which brought Bradman to the crease. His arrival produced the usual flurry of excitement in the crowd, but the excitement was short-lived. Attempting to turn Larwood to leg in the seventh over of the innings, Bradman spooned a catch to Gubby Allen, fielding at short-leg and was out for 8. It was the only time that summer that Bradman was caught in the bodyline trap.

Even before Bradman was out, however, there had occurred the first of the great shocks of the Adelaide Test. Following his usual practice, Larwood had begun bowling to an orthodox field, and he still had that field set when, with the last ball of his second over, he hit Woodfull a severe blow over the heart. Woodfull leapt off the ground as if struck by an electric charge, dropped his bat and, clutching his chest, staggered a few paces to the off-side of the wicket. Several Englishmen came to Woodfull's assistance, but Larwood was not one of them. Newsreel films of the incident show him turning quickly to take his cap from the umpire, George Hele. In a book he wrote forty years later with R. S. Whitington, *Bodyline Umpire*, Hele said he heard Jardine say to Larwood while he was still at the end of his follow-through, 'Well bowled, Harold.' In *The Larwood Story*, Larwood suggests that the remark was actually intended for the ears of the batsman at the bowler's end, Bradman. Jardine was not really being callous – he was trying to unsettle Bradman.

Although the ball which hit Woodfull was not a bouncer, it was certainly short of a length, and to most of the spectators it seemed that Larwood was at fault. Immediately there was uproar in the crowd; Larwood was hooted and jeered. This continued for a minute or two while Woodfull recovered from the blow to his chest, but then subsided when Allen began the next over, bowling to Bradman. Bradman took 6 off the over, pulling the ball only just short of a length for four. Larwood was to continue bowling at the other end, but at this point there was a development which had immense consequences for everyone concerned. Before Larwood bowled the first ball of the new over to Woodfull, Jardine moved his fieldsmen into the bodyline cordon, leaving only one man, Voce, at slip. This was only the fifth over of the innings, and Jardine did not usually place the bodyline field so early as this, when there was shine left on the ball, but Bradman had come in earlier than expected, and the aggression he showed against Allen in the previous over might have persuaded Jardine that he could not delay any longer. So Jardine might have had Bradman, not Woodfull, in mind when he changed, or agreed to change, the field at the start of Larwood's over, but the crowd did not see it that way. The assumption around the ground was that Jardine and Larwood were seeking to take advantage of Woodfull's injury – that they hoped to intimidate him more easily with a full-scale bodyline attack while he was still feeling shaken from the blow to his chest. Again there was uproar in the crowd, and Larwood was counted out as he ran in to bowl. Each stride he took was counted, 'one, two, three, four . . .', and finally, as he delivered the ball, there was a great shout of 'Out!'

Nothing the Englishmen did that summer caused wider or deeper resentment than Larwood's field change, and it was the only thing they did about which Jardine ever expressed regret. Indeed, in his book, *In Quest of the Ashes*, Jardine was careful to deny full responsibility for it. The field was switched, he said, after 'Larwood made a sign to me that he wanted a leg-side field.' Larwood, on the other hand, asserts in *The Larwood Story* that 'the skipper always changed the field over' and suggests that he, Larwood, had been ready to resume bowling to an orthodox field when the change of field was instituted. Jardine wrote:

'Had either he [Larwood] or I realized the misrepresentation to which we were to be subjected, neither would have set that particular field for that particular over. Woodfull is an old hand, and had he been "grey and groggy", as the majority of the Australian press suggested, he knew perfectly well that he had only to ask me for leave to discontinue his innings for his request to be instantly and readily granted. I do not imagine that Woodfull himself would claim that he was either grey or groggy.'

Woodfull was bowled by Allen for 22 just before 5 P.M. and returned sore, bruised and angry to the Australian dressing room, where the next scene in the drama was to be performed. Some time later, perhaps about an hour, the two English managers, Warner and

Palairet, called at the dressing room to offer their sympathy to him. This is Warner's own account of what happened:

> 'Our reception was freezing. Woodfull had just had a shower bath, and we found him with a towel wrapped around him, and the following conversation passed. We said how sorry we were, and Woodfull replied, "I don't want to see you, Mr Warner. There are two teams out there. One is trying to play cricket and the other is not." I replied, "Apart from all that, we most sincerely hope you are not too badly hurt," and he answered, "The bruise is coming out," and there certainly was a very livid mark over his heart. We then left the room.'

Poor Warner. He had come to Australia hoping to proclaim the idea of cricket's good fellowship, and here he was caught up in one of the most unpleasant rows the game had known. How he must silently have cursed Jardine for bringing the whole nasty business down on their heads. To be rebuked by an Australian captain under the circumstances which caused Woodfull to rebuke him must have been extremely distressing. In some ways, Warner was bodyline's unhappiest victim of all. Gubby Allen, when interviewed by Christopher Martin-Jenkins for the *Cricketer* in 1981, said, 'I know the unhappiness it [the bodyline affair] caused him. In fact more than once I remember him in tears in his hotel room.'

Yet wasn't Warner himself partly responsible for all that happened? Should he not have acted firmly, long before Australia, to put a stop to what Jardine was doing? Wasn't his faint-heartedness as important a factor in the affair as Jardine's lion-heartedness? Jack Fingleton reported the old Australian cricketer Clem Hill saying at the time to Warner, when Warner suggested there was nothing he could do about the bodyline problem, 'You can come down off the fence for a start, Plum.' Many have wondered since why Warner did not come down off the fence. He was the senior manager of the team, he believed bodyline was bad for the game, and he saw cricket as an important unifying and edifying influence in the Empire. For all these reasons he might have taken a stand against Jardine. Why didn't he? In the *Cricketer* interview, Gubby Allen throws some interesting light on this matter. In the first place, according to Allen, Warner did try on many occasions to persuade Jardine to abandon his bodyline strategy or at least to modify it. Jardine refused, and Warner apparently left it at that, believing he had done as much as he could be expected to do.

In the final analysis, it is the character of the man which provides the best explanation for the way Warner acted, or failed to act, in 1932–33. He was not as strong as Jardine – that was the key to it. 'He was essentially a kind, soft-hearted man,' Allen says. A telling comparison can be made with the Australian tours of England in 1921 and 1926. The team manager on both tours was the well-known administrator of the game in Sydney, Syd Smith. It is said that in 1921 the captain, Warwick Armstrong, was in charge, because he was a stronger character than Smith. In 1926 Smith was in charge, because he was a stronger character than the captain, Herbie Collins. A similar principle must have applied in 1932–33. In the *Cricketer* interview, Allen said, 'He [Warner] would always avoid a row if he could.' Such a man was unlikely to change the mind of Douglas Jardine.

The experience in the Australian dressing room had been a painful one for Warner, but at least none of the press corps had been there to witness it. Warner might have been thankful for that, but there was always a chance that an Australian player would pass the story on to a journalist. On the following day, Sunday, a rest day, Warner might therefore have been relieved to hear that most of the Australian cricket writers had gone off to play in a picnic cricket match outside Adelaide against a team from a theatre company. But late in the day the story broke. The Australian journalists returned from their outing and converged on him, clamouring for a comment on what had happened in the dressing room. Warner declined to make one, but next morning, Monday, the story was given great prominence by newspapers throughout Australia. Their accounts of the incident were detailed and generally accurate: clearly, their primary source of information had been someone who witnessed the scene.

Tom Goodman of the *Sydney Morning Herald* says he and the other journalists knew nothing of the affair until they returned from the picnic match. They found Claude Corbett of the Sydney *Sun* and R. W. E. 'Bun' Wilmot of the Melbourne *Argus*, who had remained in Adelaide all day, waiting for them at the hotel. Corbett and Wilmot announced they had got on to a sensational story which they were ready to share with them, and proceeded to relate what had occurred between Warner and Woodfull. Goodman says there had been an understanding that Corbett and Wilmot would 'mind the shop' while the others were at the cricket match – that is, that they would cover for them if anything happened – so it did not seem strange to him that they were prepared to share the story. Goodman says he had no idea then, and has no idea now, whether it was Corbett or Wilmot who first uncovered the story, or whether they had uncovered it together. Nor did he have any idea who leaked the story to them. He knew

Corbett well for many years afterwards, but never thought it proper to ask him. Warner, however, came to a conclusion at once about who was responsible for the leak. He blamed Jack Fingleton and offered Larwood a pound if he could get him out for another duck in the second innings, which Larwood managed to do. Fingleton was a professional journalist and he was one of the few Australian players in the dressing room at the time, a fact Fingleton himself confirmed. But Fingleton denied strenuously that he was responsible for the leak and said he believed Bradman was. Sir Donald has denied this just as strenuously and has said he always believed Fingleton was responsible. Only one conclusion from all this is possible: the story was leaked by a third person, whose identity seems destined to remain a mystery.

After the revelations in the newspapers on Monday morning, the atmosphere at the Adelaide Oval was noticeably tense when play began at noon. There was some speculation that morning, in the Australian dressing room and elsewhere, the Jardine might moderate his tactics as a result of Woodfull's outburst. It was thought that the unpleasant turn of events on Saturday must have caused him some concern, and that in any case Pelham Warner had surely prevailed upon him to take the heat out of the battle. But such thinking took no account of Jardine's fixity of purpose. From the very first over of the day, bowled by Larwood, Jardine made it plain that he had no intention of relenting. A bodyline field was set for that over and Larwood bowled accordingly. Ponsford, who was on 45 at stumps on Saturday, resumed his innings, and in Larwood's third over he was struck by a rising ball in the back. It was one of many blows there he received during this innings, for he had adopted the desperate policy of turning his back into the bouncers, rather than risk knocking up a catch to one of the short-legs. Ponsford went on to make 85, easily his best Test innings that season, and he says that when he got out of the shower in the dressing room afterwards Vic Richardson drew the other players' attention to a mass of bruises in the region of his left shoulder blade. Ponsford played in three Tests in 1932–33, and he estimates he was hit fifty times in all.

Ponsford had put on 63 runs in partnership with Bert Oldfield, and after he was out Oldfield continued to score freely. Oldfield batted at number seven. He was the first of the tail-enders rather than the last of the batsmen, but he could on occasions be extremely difficult to dislodge. In the Tests of 1932–33, he averaged 27.2, which was higher than the averages of Fingleton and Ponsford and nearly as high as Richardson's, yet it is questionable whether he was skilled enough with the bat to be considered fair game by a bowler of Larwood's pace in 1932–33, when the code of fair play prohibited the bowling of bouncers at tail-enders. That code has long since ceased to be observed, of course, and no fast bowler would think twice about bowling bouncers at Bert Oldfield today.

Larwood took the new ball when the score passed 200 and he bowled initially to an off-side field, but Oldfield hit him for a couple of fours, and the fieldsmen were moved into the bodyline formation. Then came the next great shock of the Adelaide Test. In trying to swing a rising ball from Larwood to leg, Oldfield was struck on the right side of his forehead. He lurched behind the stumps and collapsed on the ground. Within seconds he was surrounded by a group of Englishmen, including Larwood. Gubby Allen ran to the dressing room to fetch water and a towel, and Bill Woodfull, wearing a suit, strode out to the middle with his shoulders back, as if he were beside himself with anger. Oldfield recovered after a few minutes and was able to walk from the ground unassisted, but the 32,000 spectators could not have been more enraged by what they had seen than if Oldfield had been killed.

Probably as a result of the publicity given to the Woodfull-Warner incident, the Englishmen had been barracked savagely all day. Jardine was jeered each time he handled the ball, and once when he chased a ball to the boundary he received a great chorus of personal abuse from the adjacent section of the crowd. But Oldfield's injury raised the fury of the crowd to a level the Englishmen had not known before. Bill Ferguson remembered Maurice Tate saying to him at the time, 'Bill, I'm getting out of here. Somebody is going to get seriously hurt, and the people will start a riot.' Tate had been sitting out in the open, but now retreated to the dressing room. Ferguson felt sure some hotheads would jump the fence and try to assault the English players. Others had the same fear, including the umpires George Hele and George Borwick. In his book, *Bodyline Umpire*, Hele said:

'George Borwick and I were worried that the crowd would leap the fence and make an all-out assault on the Englishmen. I decided that, if the crowd did come, I would grab the stumps and use them to prevent myself from attack. The Englishmen kept turning towards the eastern mound to watch the crowd there while Oldfield was on the ground. Loud booing persisted from most parts of the ring and Jardine was booed individually and heckled continuously for minutes.'

Larwood wrote:

'I was frightened at how serious Bert's injury might be; I was also frightened at the abuse and barracking of the crowd. I thought they were going to come at us . . . I felt that one false move would bring the crowd down on me. I was glad when he finished off the last three batsmen and were able to go in to the comparative safety of the dressing room.'

Jardine did not express regret publicly for what had happened to Oldfield, but he did make two private gestures. First, he sent Oldfield's wife, Ruth, a telegram on behalf of the English team, in which he said that his players hoped Oldfield would recover speedily from his injury. Later, he arranged for a personal friend of his in Sydney to deliver two Shirley Temple dolls to the Oldfield home as gifts for Oldfield's two small daughters. This has been revealed only recently by Mrs Oldfield.

An X-ray found that the blow to Oldfield's forehead had caused a small fracture of the skull, and Oldfield missed the fourth Test because of it. He was generous enough, however, to absolve Larwood of any blame for the injury. 'I do not wish anyone to accept the consequences of my mistake,' he said. 'In this particular instance, Larwood was not to blame, as the ball which hit me was pitched in line with the wicket, short, and somehow I lost sight of it after the ball hit the pitch. The next thing I knew it had hit me.' He expanded on this in the book he wrote a few years later, *Behind the Wicket*. He said there was a special problem at Adelaide – the sightboards were too small. Larwood's arm when he delivered the ball, according to Oldfield, was always well above the sightboard, which made it impossible for the batsman to pick up the ball until it was well on its way towards him. 'This unquestionably caused me to lose sight of the ball when I was in the course of making my stroke,' Oldfield wrote. 'I intended to pull it as it was very short.'

Not every Australian was as willing as this to absolve Larwood from blame. True, Woodfull and Oldfield had been hit by 'fair' deliveries – that is, balls which were not short enough to be considered genuine bouncers and which had not been directed at the batsman's body. But there had been plenty of 'unfair' deliveries, too, any of which might have caused injuries at least as severe. In Sydney, a District Court judge named John Sheridan expressed the view that England's bodyline bowlers might be liable to prosecution under the *Crimes Act*:

'I gather that people contend that though body bowling is dangerous, it is not prohibited by the rules of cricket. I would suggest that it may be covered by the criminal law. By our *Crimes Act* it is a serious offence maliciously to wound a man or inflict grievous bodily harm upon him . . .'

There is evidence that Larwood did bowl at Adelaide with special aggression. Lloyd Dumas, the managing editor of the Adelaide *Advertiser* newspaper, who, as we shall see, worked hard later to try to end the ill-feeling caused by bodyline, wrote in his autobiography, *The Story of a Full Life*, that a prominent Adelaide citizen had taken the trouble to position himself behind the sightboard and count the balls which were directed at the stumps and the balls directed at the batsmen. His finding was that very nearly half, actually 34 out of 72, were aimed at the batsmen. It is Bill Ponsford's recollection that four or five balls of an (eight-ball) over when the bodyline field was set were bouncers – not necessarily head-high ones, but bouncers nevertheless. Vic Richardson said that it was at Adelaide that he tried taking guard outside the leg stump, a tactical move which certain Englishmen considered a possible answer to bodyline, but found the ball still coming at him, no matter how far he retreated to the on-side.

Perhaps Larwood bent his back more in Adelaide at Jardine's bidding, realizing that they had to keep the lid on Bradman. Perhaps he also did it in retaliation, as it were, for the abuse and jeering he had been subjected to. His Notts captain, Arthur Carr, wrote, 'The Australian crowds and newspapers played right into the hands of Larwood. They got his back up, made him angry and determined – and when you do that to Larwood you add to his effectiveness. He is stubborn by nature and the more he is goaded on the more he puts his back into his bowling.' This happened in the previous Test at Melbourne, and perhaps it happened at Adelaide. At Adelaide Larwood bowled with a grimness of intent which left no one under the impression that he was merely doing his captain's bidding. It was the speed and ferocity of his bowling there, in fact, which really brought the bodyline row to a head.

The Warner–Woodfull unpleasantness on Saturday had an unhappy sequel on this Monday. In the morning, while Ponsford was taking a beating about his shoulder blades, Warner approached the journalists sitting in a single row in front of the players' enclosures and announced happily, 'The incident concerning Woodfull and myself is now closed. He apologized for what happened in a very nice manner. We are now the best of friends.' News of Warner's statement reached the Australian camp quickly, for only an hour or two later the journalists were approached by Bill Jeanes, the secretary of both the South Australian Cricket Association and the Board of Control, who on this occasion was acting as a kind of press officer for Woodfull. Jeanes asked if it were true that Warner had claimed an apology had been made and, on being told it was, he said, 'Then Woodfull denies that any apology was ever made.' The bemused journalists went back to Warner, who insisted that what Woodfull had said to him had certainly sounded to his ears, anyway, like an apology, and there was some talk of Warner and Woodfull meeting again to resolve the matter. The meeting was actually the idea of the English journalist Bruce Harris, who may have been one of those newspapermen who like to help shape the news before they report it, and there was never any real possibility that it would take place.

In the meantime, Jeanes had conferred with Woodfull again, and later that day issued the following statement on Woodfull's behalf: 'I did not apologize to Mr Warner. I merely told him that the matter was not a personal one between him and myself. I repudiate any suggestion that I tendered an apology to him for any statement I made.' It was an unnecessary misunderstanding, and a most unfortunate one for Warner. He would have been aghast at the publicity given to the dressing-room incident in the newspapers that morning, and by hastening to tell the journalists of Woodfull's 'apology' he had obviously been trying to defuse the situation. Instead, he had achieved exactly the opposite result, and caused himself more personal embarrassment. For Warner, the real troubles were only beginning.

9
Controversy to Crisis

Some time on Monday, the day Oldfield was hit, four senior cricket officials watching the match at Adelaide resolved upon a course of action which was suddenly to turn the controversy over bodyline bowling into a crisis. They decided to send a cable of protest about Jardine's tactics to the MCC at Lord's. The four officials were the three South Australian members of the Board of Control, B. V. Scrymgeour, H. W. Hodgetts and R. F. Middleton, and one Victorian member of the Board who happened to be in Adelaide, Bill Kelly. We do not know precisely how they arrived at the decision, but we do know it was a complaint by Bill Woodfull which first persuaded them they had to do something. In the Australian Cricket Board's archives there is a letter written a few days later by Bill Jeanes, the Board of Control's secretary, which states that 'Mr Woodfull complained to Mr Warner about the tactics adopted by the MCC team and to members of the Board and myself. He expressed the opinion that the Board should take prompt action in the matter.'

Woodfull may have made this appeal to the Board as early as Saturday, when he was hit, or as late as Monday afternoon, when Oldfield was hit. It was on Monday, anyway, that the four Board members responded to it. Their first move was to hold a meeting at the ground with the English managers, Warner and Palairet, at which the two Englishmen were asked to stop their players bowling bodyline. According to

Bruce Harris, the English journalist, Warner and Palairet replied that the English team's tactics on the field were Jardine's business and that they were powerless to do anything. It was because Warner and Palairet were unable, or unwilling, to act that the four Board members decided, more in hot blood than in cold, to lock horns with the MCC itself. Perhaps it was the injury to Oldfield in the afternoon which precipitated the decision; the feelings of the Board members would have been running as high as anyone's at the time. We know the idea of sending a cable to London was conceived on Monday because Jeanes was in contact with a Tasmanian Board member, H. Bushby, about it that day. Jeanes was also in contact that day with the chairman of the Board, Dr Allen Robertson, who was in Melbourne. Robertson had taken a strong dislike to the Englishmen's bowling methods, and it is possible the idea of protesting directly to the MCC was originally his. The interesting thing about all this is that it does not seem that the Board members at any stage considered appealing to Jardine. No doubt they knew him well enough to realize how futile this would be.

Jack Fingleton makes a puzzling addition to the story in his book, *Cricket Crisis*. He wrote:

> 'The Board first tried to induce Woodfull and Bradman to put their names to a cable to the MCC and leave the Board out of it, but the two players told the Board, in effect, that as it had been elected to govern the game in Australia it, perforce, should govern and do its own cabling job. And the Board did do its own cabling job.'

Fingleton could not really have meant that the Board, as a board, made this extraordinary suggestion to Woodfull and Bradman. It could only have been one or two Board members; there is no reference at all to the matter in the Australian Cricket Board's archives. Even so, and in the absence of other evidence to support it, this episode is difficult to accept. It is possible, although unlikely, that the Board members in Adelaide might have wanted Woodfull, as captain, to endorse their cable in some way, but what possible reason could they have had for bringing Bradman into it? As he was bodyline's principal target, he ought to have been the last person the Board would have wanted to protest to the MCC about its fairness. Woodfull and Bradman did not give the matter much weight, and it need not be given much weight here.

Meanwhile, the match continued. Australia was all out for 222 on Monday afternoon, 119 behind England, and England's second innings continued on Tuesday. The atmosphere at the Adelaide Oval was so different on Tuesday that it hardly seemed the same ground. The crowd, 19,821, was much smaller and was strangely subdued. It was as if it had exhausted all its fury on Saturday and Monday. Even while Jardine was inching his way to a score of 56, his highest of the series, barrackers were heard only occasionally. It may have been during this innings of his – it was certainly during this match – that a barracker yelled at Jardine, when he brushed some flies from his face, to 'leave our flies alone'. Jardine's daughter, Mrs Lawry, says this was one remark her father always remembered with amusement. There was an unusual happening on the field late that day. Don Bradman, brought on to bowl a couple of overs just before stumps, bowled Wally Hammond with a full toss when the master batsman was only 15 short of a century. It was the only wicket Bradman ever took in a Test match.

To the forty or so journalists at the ground, however, what was happening on the field on Tuesday seemed almost incidental to what was going on behind closed doors in the grandstand. The four Board members had a meeting at the ground in the morning, and it was not long before the news leaked out that they intended sending a cable of protest to Lord's. It is likely that the purpose of that meeting on Tuesday morning was to draft the cable. We know the drafting was done by the four Board members at the ground and that it was later approved by Dr Robertson in Melbourne. There were thirteen Board members in all, and Jeanes spent much of Tuesday sending telegrams to the others to try to get majority approval for sending the cable. The four Board members in Adelaide were in favour of it and so was Dr Robertson in Melbourne, so Jeanes needed to get the agreement of only two others. In the end he did obtain the majority he was seeking, but not much more than that. The final vote was eight for and five against. New South Wales' three Board members and Queensland's two were opposed to sending the cable, and the matter was effectively decided by the one Tasmanian on the Board and the one Western Australian. The two Queenslanders believed that Woodfull should have submitted a detailed, written complaint before the Board took action.

Newspaper reports tell us that Warner had another meeting with the four Board members on Tuesday afternoon. It was probably then that he learned of their intention to send a cable of protest to Lord's. 'I ventured to suggest that we should be allowed to see the cable before it was despatched,' Warner later wrote, 'as we might possibly be able to suggest some useful phrase or word.' Warner sensed, correctly, that these four Australians were in no mood to be diplomatic. He had an intimate knowledge, as they did not, of the kind of people who ran things at Lord's. He

knew their principles and their prejudices, and he
knew that an offensive, crudely worded protest would
achieve nothing, except cause them offence. Warner's
offer to vet the text of the cable was therefore a
generous and really a very valuable one, and one that
Jeanes and the others ought to have taken advantage
of. Oddly enough, the Board members and Warner
may have had a common interest in the matter. Things
had got to such a pitch that he might not have been
averse at all to the idea of the MCC intervening and
bringing Jardine to heel, as he had been unable to
himself. Secretly, he may have been quite happy for
the cable to succeed. He was told he would have the
chance to inspect it before it was sent, but this did not
happen. A few hours later Jeanes handed him a copy
of the cable. Warner read it and said, 'This hasn't
gone, has it?', but it had. 'One does not wish to disturb
sleeping dogs,' Warner wrote some years afterwards,
'but this cable was scarcely couched in diplomatic terms
. . . Australia had a good case, but they spoilt it in
their presentation of it to an English jury, who reacted
on the lines of "my country, right or wrong".' One
wonders how differently things might have turned out
if Warner had been given the chance to 'suggest some
useful phrase or word' before the cable was sent. Of
all the might-have-beens in the bodyline story, this is
one of the most interesting.

The cable was eventually sent at 3.12 P.M. on Wednesday, 18 January the second-last day of the Test,
which means it was roughly two days in the making.
Although it was conceived in haste it was not, as some
of its critics later suggested, despatched in haste. The
main reason for the delay, probably, was that Jeanes
had trouble contacting the far-flung Board members.
Why was it not shown to Warner as agreed? A possible

explanation is that Jeanes and the others had taken so long to get the cable ready for transmission that they did not dare risk a further delay by showing it to him, for Warner was bound to find fault with it. The cable was relying for much of its impact on the injuries Woodfull and more particularly Oldfield had suffered, and the fresher those injuries were in the minds of the people at Lord's, the greater the impact the cable would make on them. Moreover, Australia was clearly heading for defeat in the Test, and it was obviously preferable that a protest about England's tactics should be made before those tactics resulted in victory. On the day the cable was sent, Australia was still officially level with England in the series, at one Test all. For all these reasons, the Board could not delay the cable any longer.

The cable read:

> 'Bodyline bowling has assumed such proportions as to menace the best interests of the game, making protection of the body by the batsmen the main consideration. This is causing intensely bitter feeling between the players, as well as injury. In our opinion, it is unsportsmanlike. Unless stopped at once, it is likely to upset the friendly relations between Australia and England.'

This, then, was the result of the Board's labours from Monday to Wednesday. It is probably the most famous document in the history of Anglo-Australian sport, so great were its repercussions and potential repercussions, and it has been analysed, word by word, on countless occasions since it was released to the Australian press on the same afternoon it was sent to London.

What can we make of it today, so many years later? The word 'unsportsmanlike' jars now as it did then,

when both Jardine and the authorities at Lord's took
such exception to it, yet it did describe quite accurately
the Australian attitude to bodyline bowling. Australians really did consider bodyline unsportsmanlike, and
for the Board to have said less might have been tactful
but it would not have been the truth. The very first
word in the cable, 'bodyline', does not jar now, but it
certainly did at Lord's in 1933. As we shall see, it was
a word which the Board refrained entirely from using
in later dealings with the MCC. Finally, there is the
extravagant statement in the last sentence that bodyline
was placing relations between Britain and Australia at
risk. Did the authors of the cable mean what they
actually said here, or did they mean simply that
relations between the two countries was at risk so far
as cricket was concerned? We must assume it was the
former; if it had been the latter the ambiguity of it
would surely have been obvious to them. It must be
remembered that the Board members who composed
the cable had witnessed extremely ugly crowd scenes
at Adelaide, and they might easily have concluded that
the ill-feeling caused by bodyline was extending beyond
the game, which up to a point was true.

There is one question about the cable which deserves
a re-examination after all these years. What was the
Board's real purpose in sending it? Was the cable a
genuine request for intervention by the MCC? Did the
Board really hope that, upon receiving it, the MCC
would act to stop bodyline 'at once', as the cable
demanded? Or was the cable more in the nature of a
gesture? Was the Board for the moment simply sound-
ing off, giving vent to the rage of millions of Australians, in expectation of coming to terms with the MCC
about bodyline some time in the future? If it were the
latter, and the probability is that it was, it would

explain why the cable was not worded more diplomatically. A letter which the Board's chairman, Dr Robertson, wrote to Bill Jeanes on 23 January, when they were still awaiting the MCC's reply to the cable, gives an insight into his thinking at least:

'The players I have seen or heard of are all very sympathetic in their protest. I've only spoken to Woodfull on the phone, but I understand he is very disgusted and annoyed with the English methods. My own personal feeling in the matter is that I would go so far as to cancel the next Test games and all Test games for the next ten or twelve years, but of course I am only one of the number. Am wondering what the MCC Committee will do. Fancy that they might probably ask Warner & Co for their version before finally deciding or perhaps they might take up the attitude that they must leave matters in the hands of their captain.'

The tone of this letter suggests that Robertson was not hopeful of receiving a satisfactory reply from Lord's. On the contrary, he was obviously looking ahead to a protracted wrangle with the MCC. 'I am ready for the fray,' he told Jeanes.

The shutters went up around the English camp as soon as the cable was sent. Newspaper reporters badgered Pelham Warner for a comment about it, but he steadfastly refused to give them one, on one occasion adding that, like Bismark, he could remain silent in seven languages. Jardine was as inaccessible to the Australian press as always, so Australians had no idea how he was reacting personally to the new crisis. In fact, he was worried – not because feelings were running so high against him in Australia but because he feared the MCC would not support him. He confessed this to Gubby Allen at the time. Allen recalls:

'I remember Douglas saying to me, "Have you seen the cable?" And I said, "Yes, I have – it's awful." He said, "That word unsportsmanlike . . ." I said, "Douglas, you're absolutely wrong. That's the best thing that could have happened." He said, "No, they'll let me down at Lord's." And I said, "Douglas, no one can call an Englishman unsporting and get away with it. They'll back you to the hilt." I can still see the smile that came over his face. He thought I'd perhaps hit the nail on the head.'

Jardine had one other cause for discomfort. Several Australian newspapers had published stories in the previous few days suggesting that the bodyline affair had created a rift in the English team, the suggestion being that some of the English players were opposed to Jardine's methods. On Wednesday evening, a few hours after the Board had sent its cable, the Englishmen held a team meeting at their hotel at Glenelg, at the end of which they agreed unanimously to a resolution denying there had been dissension and reaffirming their loyalty to Jardine. This is Jardine's account of how the meeting came to be held:

'After the behaviour of the crowd at Adelaide, and in view of the tone of a large section of the Australian press, I deemed it wise that the whole side should have an opportunity of meeting and discussing leg-theory. In order, further, that they should do so with complete freedom, I made it clear that I did not attend the meeting myself . . . I felt exceedingly strongly that unless the team was wholeheartedly convinced of its own rectitude and sportsmanship, the enjoyment of the tour (which is a vital factor in efficiency) would have been so seriously impaired that, solely for the sake of that efficiency, I should have been prepared to consider the abandonment of leg-theory.'

Notwithstanding Jardine's obscure references to enjoyment and efficiency, the meaning of this last sentence is clear: he was ready to abandon his bowling tactics if his team had misgivings about them. By now Jardine knew that two of his players, Allen and Pataudi, were opposed to them, and he may well have guessed that his vice-captain, Wyatt, and possibly one of the junior team members, Freddie Brown, were unhappy about them, too. But these four, apparently, joined with the other players that night in pledging loyalty to Jardine and support for what he was doing. The Board's cable, and especially 'that word' unsportsmanlike, had made them close ranks around the man the cable was meant to condemn.

The Test ended, to the relief of many, on the Thursday. England made 412 in its second innings, setting Australia 532 to win. England's second innings ended at 3.21 P.M. on Wednesday – nine minutes after the Board sent its cable to Lord's – and Woodfull and Fingleton came to the crease to embark on what was clearly an impossible task. Larwood bowled Fingleton for a duck in his second over, thereby earning the pound note Warner had promised him. It was Fingleton's second duck of the match and it cost him his place in the team for the rest of the series. A season which began with so much promise for him had ended in crushing disappointment. Fingleton's first three Test scores had been 26, 40 and 83, and his last three had been 1, 0 and 0. He had fought gallantly, but was overwhelmed in the end. Fingleton was replaced by Ponsford, who almost immediately hit a catch to Jardine in the gully, bringing Don Bradman to the crease.

As usual, Larwood had begun bowling to an orthodox field. It had been normal practice for him to move his slips across to the bodyline cordon after his third over, and when in this innings he began bowling his fourth over to an orthodox field he was widely applauded by the crowd. Bradman came in during this over, but Larwood still made no move to switch the field to the leg-side. When he began his fifth over still bowling to an orthodox field, he was generously applauded again. There was a buzz of speculation about the ground: was it possible the Englishmen had yielded to public pressure and forsaken their leg-theory tactics? For his sixth over, too, Larwood maintained the off-side field, but before the start of his seventh over the hated manoeuvre took place: all but one slip moved into the leg-side trap. At once there was a storm of abuse from the crowd, and Larwood was again counted out as he ran in to bowl, just as he had been in the first innings.

Up to this moment Bradman's batting had been bright but steady. As soon as the bodyline field was placed, we are told, his batting took on a different character. One newspaper said it seemed as if he had decided to do or die. This was the first of a series of brilliant, unorthodox, daring innings which Bradman played during that series in his counter-attack against bodyline bowling. Newspaper reports tell us that some of his shots were so audacious they made the crowd gasp, and a typical example was cutting Larwood off his leg stump. 'Only a batsman with phenomenal sight and footwork could do that,' Larwood wrote.

Bradman also made the most of any respite from bodyline, and he attacked the bowling of Verity and Hammond with urgency whenever they were brought on. He made several spectacular assaults on Verity in particular. 'I thought I had better hit Verity before Larwood hit me,' Bradman was reported to have said. In this innings, after racing to 50 in only 64 minutes, he pulled Verity to the boundary twice in quick succession, and then swung him to leg for six. The ball hit a woman sitting in front of the grandstand on the arm, and she was later treated by ambulance officers. But immediately afterwards Bradman was out, going down the wicket to loft Verity over mid-off and instead hitting a catch back to the bowler. Having kept the lion at bay, Bradman fell prey to the lamb. In only 73 minutes he had scored 66 of an Australian total of 86.

Bradman's unconventional batting thrilled the crowds but it did not impress all the critics or, it seems, all his team-mates. In *Cricket Crisis*, Fingleton said, 'Bradman's playing of bodyline did not make it any easier for the other Australian batsmen.' The implication here, apparently, is that the team's outstanding batsman should have given a lead which the other batsmen were capable of following. None of the others, not even McCabe, could hope to play bodyline as Bradman was trying to play it – they did not possess the speed, the eyesight or the footwork to do so. It is clear there was some resentment, too, at the fact that Bradman was not being hit by the bouncers as the others were. (In fact, he was hit only once in the series – by Larwood in the fifth Test.) After Bradman was caught in the bodyline trap off Larwood in the first innings at Adelaide, the *Sydney Morning Herald* reported an unnamed Australian player as saying, 'Don should have taken that on the body to be absolutely safe.'

Bradman's team-mates were well aware that bodyline was invented for Bradman, and it may have rankled with them that they, not he, were taking most of bodyline's blows. There are several allusions to this in Fingleton's writing. 'Where I think Jardine made his mistake,' he once wrote, 'was in thinking that the Australian eleven was made up of 11 Bradmans.' This was not Bradman's fault, of course, but it would have been contrary to human nature if it did not influence to some degree the way his team-mates viewed his batting methods.

Of course, the matter acquires a completely different complexion when it is viewed from Bradman's angle. It was surely absurd to expect him to stand in the line of the ball and be hit by Larwood in order to provide some kind of inspiration for his team-mates. It is to Bradman's great credit that he did try something different to combat bodyline, that he did try to wrest the initiative from Jardine, that he did not bow to the inevitable. He was aware of the criticism of his tactics and he resented it. 'Apparently I had to make a century every time and also be hit more often than anyone else to satisfy the tastes of some,' he wrote.

At the start of play on Thursday, Australia was 4 for 120. It lost its last six wickets for 73 runs, which meant England was the victor by the huge margin of 338 runs. Apart from Bradman, the only other Australian to emerge from the innings with honour was Woodfull, who carried his bat in making 73, which was to be his highest score of the series. Larwood and Allen each took four wickets, raising their totals for the match to seven and eight respectively. Thus, the most successful English bowler in the match which made bodyline an international talking point was a bowler who never once bowled bodyline.

In England, as in Australia, the Board of Control's cable was the news of the hour, and there was much speculation about the kind of response the MCC would eventually make to it. Most British newspapers urged the MCC to reject the Australian protest out of hand. They accused Australians of being squealers, a word which gained a lot of currency in England in the following months. A *Daily Herald* editorial said,

'Ninety per cent of the cricket followers in England will label the protest as squealing. Are they far wrong?' The former England captain Lord Tennyson said in the *Evening Standard*, 'Play the game, Australia, stop squealing.' Percy Fender said in the *Daily Telegraph*, 'It is a pity that so much thought has been wasted in finding the new name, bodyline bowling, for something as old as the hills.'

Yet there were some in England who were able to see the Australian point of view. Sir Stanley Jackson, a former England captain and a man of influence in the game, said, 'I firmly believe that if it became common for fast bowlers to use this method of attack it would ruin the game.' E. A. McDonald, the Australian fast bowler of the early 1920s, who had been living for some years in England, said:

'I am decidedly against bodyline bowling. If [Jack] Gregory and I were over there we would stop it by retaliation. If they hurt one of our players I would do likewise . . . Gregory and I are hailed as the originators of bodyline bowling, but we are straight up-and-downers and bowled to an ordinary field.'

In fact, there were occasions in England when McDonald did bowl to a leg-theory field. However, the most interesting of the supporters of the Australian position was Frank Foster, the pre-war English leg-theory bowler, whom Jardine had consulted about leg-side field placings before he left for Australia. Foster told the Australian Press Association on the day the cable was sent:

'There is such a thing in cricket as sportsmanship. The English team is not showing the true spirit. For Larwood to adopt leg bowling theory and for Voce to do so over the wicket is not only against the ethics of true sportsmanship but is a sign of weakness. Larwood is far too good to resort to leg-theory.'

10

Rebuff from Lord's

The MCC Committee which met on Monday, 23 January to consider the Board of Control's protest was a much-titled, very elite body. Among its twenty-two members were the Duke of Buccleuch, the Earl of Lucan, the Earl of Dartmoor, Viscount Lewisham, Viscount Ullswater, Viscount Bridgeman, Viscount Hampden, Lord Hawke, Lord Aberdare, various knights and a number of distinguished cricketers of the past, including L. C. H. Palairet, the brother of the English team's co-manager, Percy Chapman, who had captained the MCC in Australia four years before, and, although absent, Pelham Warner. These were men who had absolute confidence in the pre-eminence of the MCC in cricket. They would not easily be intimidated by an angry cable from Australia, particularly one which accused their players of being bad sportsmen, an accusation that cast aspersions on the MCC itself. The MCC's reply, therefore, was by and large predictable. It read:

'We, Marylebone Cricket Club, deplore your cable. We deprecate your opinion that there has been unsportsmanlike play. We have fullest confidence in captain, team and managers, and are convinced that they would do nothing to infringe either the laws of cricket, or the spirit of the game. We have no evidence that our confidence has been misplaced. Much as we regret accidents to Woodfull and Oldfield, we understand that in neither case was the bowler to blame. If the Australian Board of Control wish to propose a new law or rule, it shall receive our careful consideration in due course. We hope the situation is not now as serious as your cable would seem to indicate, but if it is such as to jeopardize the good relations between English and Australian cricketers, and you consider it desirable to cancel remainder of programme, we would consent, but with great reluctance.'

The MCC had not only called the Board's bluff, it had effectively raised the stakes. Whereas the Board's cable had spoken vaguely about some undefined harm that might be done to Anglo-Australian relations, the MCC's reply warned of a consequence that was real and immediate – the cancellation of the rest of the tour. The MCC no doubt hoped that this prospect would alarm the Board and put it on the defensive. In an editorial next day, *The Times* of London said the MCC had held out an olive branch in its reply to the Board. In fact, the MCC's reply was a total rebuff for the Board. It rejected all of the Board's complaints and made not a single concession. Moreover, the Board was entitled to take personal offence from the fourth sentence – 'We have no evidence that our confidence has been misplaced' – for it was tantamount to saying that the observations and opinions of the most senior cricket administrators in Australia, as stated in the Board's cable, were not worthy to be accepted as evidence. The MCC's message was plain enough: the Board had to back down.

Could the MCC Committee have reacted to the Board's protest in any other way? Was it not wholly unreasonable of the Board to expect the people at Lord's, 20,000 kilometres away, to disown their captain on the strength of a sixty-two-word telegram? As Eric Barbour commented at the time, the Board could scarcely have stated its case convincingly in a telegram of 1,000 words. The Board's protest really only had one hope of success, and that was if Pelham Warner had in some way supported it.

Warner must have been in contact with the MCC many times, both by telephone and telegram, in the five days between the sending of the Board's protest and the sending of the MCC's reply. He disliked Jardine's leg-theory, he was horrified by the bitterness it was causing in Australia and, in his own words, he thought the Board had a 'good case' to put to the MCC, if only it had gone the right way about putting it. Yet it does not seem that Warner said a word of all this to the MCC during those five crucial days. If the senior English team manager had reported to Lord's that bodyline was bad for cricket and that something needed to be done about it, the MCC Committee would hardly have reacted to the Board's protest as it did. Why did Warner not speak up? Perhaps once more he was simply taking the soft option. Perhaps, too, he was so outraged by the word 'unsportsmanlike' that for the moment he was intent only on defending Jardine. Whatever the reason for it, Warner's apparent failure to report to Lord's on the situation as he saw it had greater consequences than anything else he did, or failed to do, that summer.

The Board responded to the MCC in a second cable on 30 January. This was a composition altogether different from the previous one. It was drafted and approved by a full meeting of the Board in Sydney, its text was not released to the press in Australia until it had been received at Lord's, and it was moderate in language and conciliatory in tone. In it, the Board retracted its claim that bodyline bowling had to be stopped 'at once' to prevent a rupture in relations between England and Australia, and instead indicated that it was prepared to wait until the following season to have the matter dealt with. But it did not retract its claim that the Englishmen's bowling methods were 'unsportsmanlike'. The cable said:

> 'We appreciate your difficulty in dealing with this matter without having seen the actual play. We unanimously regard bodyline bowling, as adopted in some games in the present tour, as opposed to the spirit of cricket, and unnecessarily dangerous to the players. We are deeply concerned that the ideals of the game shall be preserved, and we have therefore appointed a committee to report on the means necessary to eliminate such bowling from Australian cricket, beginning with the 1933–34 season. We will forward its recommendations for your consideration and hope for your co-operation in their application to all cricket. We do not consider it necessary to cancel the remainder of the programme.'

The Board's second cable received qualified approval in England, if newspaper comments may be taken as a guide. Some of the comments were critical. The *Evening Standard*, for instance, said in an editorial, 'The Board's reply is ungracious, and positively sulky. It makes no amends for the uncouthness and untimeliness of the original cable.' The *Star*, on the other hand, considered the second cable to be a great leap towards reasonableness. 'We have heard the voice of the barracker, and now we hear the voice of cricket statesmanship,' it said. The cable did have a problem, though, and it was *The Times* which identified it most succinctly. 'Although the Board no longer describe bodyline bowling as unsportsmanlike,' *The Times* said, 'they still in effect bring the same charge against the English captain of the team by recording their conviction that it is contrary to the spirit of the game. This is a distinction without a difference.'

The members of the MCC Committee might have been prepared to tolerate that distinction, but far away in Australia Jardine was not so prepared. After the charge of unsportsmanlike play was made in the Board's first cable, Jardine had let it be known that he would not captain England in the two remaining Tests if there was not a retraction in the meantime. The first of these, the fourth Test in Brisbane, was due to start on 10 February. 'I was firmly determined that I should not lead them on to the field of play in another Test match, unless and until that charge had been withdrawn,' Jardine later wrote. 'I made no secret of this.' Warner had hoped the Board would make the retraction Jardine wanted in its second cable, but it did not do so. Just when it seemed to Warner that the skies were clearing, another storm, even darker than before, had rolled in.

11

A Secret Intervention

One of the most interesting intrigues in the bodyline affair did not come to light until the late 1970s – namely, a secret intervention by the Prime Minister of the day, Joseph Lyons. There had long been rumours of intervention of some kind by the Australian Government, apparently at a very high level. Jardine referred to those rumours in the book he wrote about the series, *In Quest of the Ashes*, but professed to know no more about it. Lyons himself was questioned about it at the time, but laughed it off. Warner, in his many references to the 1932–33 tour in the years that followed, does not seem to have once referred to it, which suggests that he may have been under some obligation to keep the matter in camera. It might have remained in camera, at least for some time yet, if a Canberra historian named Dr Brian Stoddart had not unearthed the diary of the British Government's representative in Australia, Ernest Crutchley. Stoddart had begun to take a professional interest in the bodyline controversy in the mid-1970s, believing it provided an enlightening study in Anglo-Australian relations, particularly insofar as those relations affected the bonds of Empire. He soon came to suspect that senior people in the Australian Government had been mixed up in the affair, and he began a long investigation to try to confirm it.

Stoddart did not follow the Crutchley lead blindly. It was well known and widely reported at the time that Warner and Palairet had approached Crutchley for help in getting the Board of Control to withdraw the charge against the English team of unsportsmanlike play, and that Crutchley had gone through Australian Government channels to do so. But nothing more than that was known. Crutchley was a man with a long and distinguished record in the service of the British Government. He was a public servant rather than a diplomat by background, and had worked for the Post Office before the war and the Department of Transport after it. He was posted to Australia in 1928 as the British Government's representative in matters of immigration, and in May 1931, he was appointed the British Government's representative in Australia proper, pending the appointment of Britain's first High Commissioner in Australia. By a coincidence, he had returned to Australia in late 1932 on the same ship which brought the English team to Australia, and we may take it for granted that he came into close contact with Warner during the voyage. Warner may have known him before then, of course. He suggests in one of his books that he knew a G. E. V. Crutchley, who may have been a relative.

Crutchley was a man of his time. He had great faith in the ties that bound Australia and Britain. In July 1931, he said in an address to the Canberra Legacy Club:

> 'Let us get together and keep together, and never drift apart. We are of the same stock; we share the same ideals. Let us march forward, side by side, helping each other over the rough patches and sharing the good things when they come – a Commonwealth of nations with a commonwealth of interests and affections.'

A man who held these views would certainly have been alarmed by the developments in the cricket world in late January 1933.

In 1978 Stoddart succeeded in tracking down the diary Crutchley kept during the summer of 1932–33, as well as copies of correspondence he had at the time with Pelham Warner. In doing so he added a new and fascinating chapter to the bodyline story. The Crutchley material revealed that in those first few, tense days of February there had been a flurry of political activity behind the scenes in Australia, extending to the Prime Minister's office itself, with the object of finding a peaceful solution to the cricket dispute. Crutchley was drawn into the row on 1 February. This was the day after the text of the Board's second cable was released and was found not to contain the retraction of the 'unsportsmanlike' charge which Warner had been counting on. Suddenly it must have seemed to Warner that the rest of the series was at real risk. Jardine was an intractable man; if he said he would not play without a retraction by the Board, he would not play. Warner also knew that the Board was in no mood to make further concessions. And if Jardine did not play, the rest of his team would certainly not play either. The remainder of the tour would be abandoned, with consequences too dreadful to contemplate. It might mean the end of Test cricket between England and Australia for four, six or even ten years, who could tell? Warner was faced with an impasse, and in desperation he decided to appeal for help to the one authority in the land which the Board of Control might be prepared to show deference to, the Australian Government.

Warner did not approach the Australian Government himself; he did not have the wherewithal to do that successfully. Instead, he did the sensible thing, and prevailed upon his new, or perhaps old, acquaintance Ernest Crutchley to make the approach for him. On 1

February he and Palairet sent Crutchley at Canberra the following telegram: 'Have under consideration cancellation of remaining matches of tour including Test owing to failure of Board to withdraw stigma of word unsportsmanlike in their first cable. Beg you use your influence to get word withdrawn. Matter very urgent.' Warner and Palairet did not suggest in so many words that Crutchley should use his influence with the Australian Government – that would have been presumptuous of them, but it was certainly what they expected him to do, and it is precisely what he did do, on the same day. Whether they knew Crutchley would go right to the top, to the Prime Minister, is another matter. Crutchley would have made it his business by now to be on familiar terms with Lyons, and he would have known that Lyons took a keen interest in cricket. He therefore decided to ask Lyons himself to put pressure on the Board of Control to withdraw its suggestion that the Englishmen's tactics were unsportsmanlike. In his diary entry for that day Crutchley wrote:

> 'I phoned the PM at Melbourne. He said to start with, "It looks as though we [are] leading two opposing armies." I told him exactly what had happened and he agreed that the cancellation of the tour would be a very grave thing, for Australia especially, just when feeling was so good. He promised to get hold of Dr Robertson, chairman of the Board of Control, and see what could be done.'

Crutchley gave a fuller account of his approach to Lyons in a letter he wrote to Warner on the following day, 2 February. Lyons made the interesting disclosure to him that he had already 'tried his hand at peacemaking' in the affair. Unfortunately, we have no way of knowing what form this earlier intervention by

Lyons took. When Crutchley asked Lyons if he would use his influence with the Board, Lyons asked in return if some gesture from the English side was possible, to which Crutchley replied that a modification of the leg-side field was not unlikely. Lyons then contacted Robertson and persuaded him to try to get the other Board members to agree to withdrawing the word 'unsportsmanlike'.

Lyons must have held out before Robertson the possibility that Jardine would moderate his tactics, for later that day he got back to Crutchley seeking confirmation from Warner that the bodyline field would be modified if the Board withdrew the word 'unsportsmanlike'. Warner personally would have been happy to give such an undertaking. In a letter to Crutchley a few days before, on 27 January, he had said, 'If we modify the placing of the field slightly for the so-called leg-theory, I do not think there will be any trouble.' It was probably on the strength of this that Crutchley told the Prime Minister that a modification of the bodyline field was not unlikely. However, Warner had been expressing merely his own opinion. The man who made the decisions, Douglas Jardine, had no intention of modifying his tactics and was beyond persuasion in the matter. Warner, therefore, had to tell Crutchley that no condition could be attached to the withdrawal of the word. Crutchley had to pass on this information, no doubt with some embarrassment, to Lyons, and Lyons, perhaps with even greater embarrassment, had to pass it on to Robertson.

Lyons used leverage of another kind to get Robertson on side. Our source of information here is a telegram Robertson sent to Jeanes on 1 February, which has been preserved in the Australian Cricket Board's archives. Robertson said:

'Prime Minister interviewed me today. Stated that British representative had seen him and asked him to get us to withdraw word objected to. If not likelihood of England pulling right out. If we do withdraw has no doubt attack will be modified. Government afraid successful conversions endangered.'

The 'conversions' Robertson refers to here were Australia's so-called conversion loans from Britain, actually old loans converted, or renegotiated, to allow easier repayment. They were of enormous importance to the Australian economy during the Depression, and any interference with them might have had the most serious consequences, a point which Lyons no doubt made strongly in his conversation with Robertson.

Of the many extraordinary scenes in the bodyline story, none is more extraordinary than the one we have here – an Australian Prime Minister negotiating with a senior British diplomat over an England cricket captain's field placings. It illustrates just how important cricket was to Australians in 1933 and, as a consequence of this, the depth of national feeling about Jardine's tactics. Lyons would have considered himself to be acting in the national interest, not just in the interests of prominent cricket officials, or even in the interests of the game as a whole. It should be noted that he did not seek to gain any political kudos from his intervention; on the contrary, he was at pains from the beginning to keep his involvement a secret.

We are left to speculate whether Lyons really believed the situation to be as serious as he described it to Robertson. Did he really believe the conversion loans to be in danger? If so, who told him so? Had he perhaps received a warning from Australia House in London about the loans? The answers to these and other questions might have been found in a file opened at the time by the Prime Minister's Department under the heading English Cricket Team 1932 – an indication, incidentally, that the file was opened in 1932, that is, before the second Test. The file's catalogue number was 748/1/291. Unfortunately, the file has disappeared, without trace and without explanation.

In England, coincidentally, there was political lobbying of a similar kind. In this case the lobbyist was the Governor of South Australia, Sir Alexander Hore-Ruthven, an Englishman and a cricket enthusiast. Hore-Ruthven had welcomed the MCC team to Adelaide on their first visit to the city, but he was on leave in London when the upheavals occurred during the third Test. After the Test, the acting Governor, Sir George Murray, arranged a meeting between Pelham Warner and several leading citizens of Adelaide, including Lloyd Dumas of the *Advertiser*, who were worried about the harm being done to Anglo-Australian relations. According to Dumas, Warner told them that he personally condemned what was happening but that on the field Jardine was in complete control. It was decided at the meeting that a report should be sent to Hore-Ruthven in London, informing him of the gravity of the situation in Australia and asking him to do what he could to help smooth things over at that end.

Hore-Ruthven acted as decisively as Crutchley did in Australia one day later. On 31 January he went to see the Dominions Secretary, Jimmy Thomas, a senior minister in the British Cabinet, and, according to press reports, spoke to Thomas about the need to ensure that relations between Australia and England were not damaged by the controversy over bodyline bowling. As a result of Hore-Ruthven's visit, Thomas called a number of MCC Committee men to his office for a conference about the matter on the following day, February 1. We do not know what was said at the meeting, but it is safe to assume that Thomas implored the MCC men to try to settle their differences with the Australian Board quickly and amicably. Hore-Ruthven attended this meeting, too, but when asked later about the part he had played said only, 'My part in the negotiations was purely personal and informal, due to a desire to help in smoothing out the cricket troubles.' The *Daily Express* in London ridiculed Thomas's intrusion into what it regarded as simply a cricket controversy. It said:

'We thought the Test farce had reached the climax with the solemn warning that relations between Britain and Australia were being endangered. Mr Thomas and MCC representatives, however, by gathering at No 10 Downing Street, heaped absurdity upon the ridiculous. There is only one thing to do now – cancel the remaining matches and bring the team home, and let the outside world enjoy the biggest laugh of a century.'

On 2 February, the day after the MCC Committee members met Jimmy Thomas, the MCC sent its reply to the Board's second cable. It said:

'We, the Committee of the Marylebone Cricket Club, note with pleasure that you do not consider it necessary to cancel the remainder of the programme, and that you are postponing the whole issue until after the present tour is completed. May we accept this as a clear indication that the good sportsmanship of our team is not in question? We are sure you will appreciate how impossible it would be to play any Test match in the spirit we all desire unless both sides were satisfied there was no reflection upon their sportsmanship. When your recommendation reaches us it shall receive our most careful consideration and will be submitted to the Imperial Cricket Conference.'

Although this was much friendlier in its tone than the MCC's previous message, its real purpose was to remind the Board that a withdrawal of the word 'unsportsmanlike' was still awaited. It is likely the MCC was not seeking the retraction for its own satisfaction, but for Jardine's. The fourth Test was now little more than a week away, and Jardine was still insisting he would not play without the retraction. By this time the English team had arrived in Brisbane to play Queensland, and there was a plaintive quality about an appeal Warner made there on 3 February in an address at a team reception:

> 'Stretch out your right hand to us and we shall grasp it eagerly. Not only will we grasp it eagerly, but every cricketer in England – I go further, every cricketer in the rest of the world – will grasp it just as certainly, because England and Australia are the great cricketing powers . . . You may think I talk too sentimentally, but I assure you I talk from the bottom of my heart. I love cricket. I adore cricket. All I can say is that I hope and pray that the sky is clearing and that the stars are appearing in the firmament of cricket. England and Australia must never be away from one another. I do ask everybody here to do everything they can in their power. I ask all men of good sense and good temper and goodwill to do everything they can to get things right at the present day.'

He concluded his address by saying, 'I believe I said that the stars would shine in a very short time. I can assure everyone that I pray for peace as much as I ever prayed for peace when my country was in danger of war.' By 6 February he was hopeful but still worried. In a letter he wrote to Crutchley on that day he said, 'I hope it will come right. We can't play if "unsportsmanlike" is not withdrawn and MCC will order us home.'

The suspense was not ended until 8 February, only two days before the Test. Late that day the Board's chairman, Dr Robertson, released the text of a cable the Board had just sent to the MCC. It read:

> 'We do not regard the sportsmanship of your team as being in question. Our position was fully considered at the recent Sydney meeting, and is as indicated in our cable of 30 January. It is the particular class of bowling referred to therein which we consider not in the best interests of cricket, and in this view we understand we are supported by many eminent English cricketers. We join heartily with you in hoping the remaining Tests will be played with the traditional good feelings.'

This was not so abject a withdrawal as it might at first glance have seemed. It might even be argued it was not a withdrawal at all. The offending assertion in the Board's original cable was that bodyline bowling was unsportsmanlike. All the Board said in this last cable was that the sportsmanship of the English players themselves was not in doubt and that the Board objected only to their bowling methods. This could be interpreted as meaning that while the Board did not regard the English players as bad sportsmen it still regarded their bowling as unsportsmanlike.

According to press reports next day, some of the English players interpreted the Board's cable in precisely that way. The important thing was that Jardine was satisfied. On the evening the text of the cable was released, he had a twelve-minute conversation with someone in London by radio-telephone. We may surmise he spoke to someone from Lord's about the cable. If he was hesitating about accepting the Board's retraction, perhaps what was said to him on the phone that night helped him make up his mind. He did not need to announce he had accepted the retraction; his appearance on the field in the fourth Test made it clear that he had. In his book about the series, he wrote, 'Personally, I was quite content to have the Board's retraction in good time instead of being left with a half-hearted apology on the morning of the match, when one might have been left in considerable doubt whether it would be accepted or not.'

The Board's third cable to the MCC ended the exchange between them which had begun exactly three weeks before. The cables had caused strife and turmoil in the cricket world and had exposed such bitter feelings generally that Government leaders in both countries felt it necessary to intervene. But at the end of it all, the Board seemed to have accomplished very little in practical terms. The MCC had made no concessions whatever, apart from agreeing to consider recommendations from the Board on the matter later that year, which was hardly a concession at all, and Jardine's men continued to bowl bodyline as purposefully as ever. Yet the Board's cables did achieve this much – they demonstrated to the English cricketers and to the English cricket authorities that Jardine's tactics were disapproved of not just by the rough-necked barrackers who shouted abuse from the public grandstands but by responsible men with a great knowledge of and devotion to the game – indeed, by the men who controlled cricket in Australia. Australia had a grievance, and the cables got that grievance off the nation's chest. They brought the row over bodyline into the open and they brought it to a head, and if this had not happened in the first two months of 1933 it would have had to happen at some other time, perhaps during the 1934 Australian tour of England, when the consequences might have been even more serious.

12

A Kind of Peace

When the Board of Control made peace with the MCC in its final cable, it seemed to bring a kind of peace, too, to the playing arena. In the fourth Test which began two days later, Larwood bowled bodyline as enthusiastically as ever (an ankle injury kept Voce out of this Test), but his bowling did not produce nearly so fierce a reaction from the Brisbane crowds as it did in Adelaide, Melbourne and, to a lesser extent, Sydney. As always, he was jeered and cat-called when he first switched the fieldsmen to the leg-side, but for the most part the crowd at the Gabba watched impassively. The fact is that bodyline, as a public issue, was by now suffering from over-exposure. The newspapers had been full of it for seven or eight weeks, and it is only natural that Australians should at last have begun to tire of it. The controversy over the cables had heightened public interest for a time, but this had fizzled now into nothing. If public interest were to be restored to its previous level, it would probably take a double-century by Don Bradman to do it.

In the weeks leading up to the fourth Test, the Australian newspapers were working on a new angle to the story. They reported that the Aboriginal fast bowler Eddie Gilbert might bowl bodyline against the Englishmen when they played Queensland in Brisbane. Gilbert, then twenty-four years old, had made a name for himself in the previous season by knocking the bat from Don Bradman's hands before getting him out for a duck. According to Bradman, this was the fastest bowling he ever encountered. Bradman survived six balls from Gilbert that day. He almost fell over backwards trying to avoid the first, had the bat knocked from his hands by the second, swung and missed at the next two, was struck on the body trying to hook the fifth and was out, caught behind, off the sixth. Bradman wrote later that the wicketkeeper who caught him was standing half-way between the stumps and boundary and yet still took the ball over his head. Bradman is said to have remarked when he returned to the dressing room that it was the luckiest duck he ever made. But despite his terrific pace and his periodic success in Sheffield Shield cricket, Gilbert was never considered a Test prospect, the reason being that he was widely believed to throw. His run to the wicket itself invited suspicion, for, as Bradman described it, he shuffled only about four quick steps before delivering the ball. His action was said to be flail-like and whippy. Nevertheless, he was by a long way the fastest bowler Australia had, at least for the few overs he was able to maintain his pace, and if the Australians ever wanted to retaliate by bowling bodyline at the Englishmen Gilbert might have seemed to some the man best able to do it for them.

On the Saturday of the Adelaide Test, the day Woodfull was hit by Larwood, Gilbert took six wickets for five runs, all of them by hitting the stumps, in a match in the Cherbourg mission area, where he lived. This performance encouraged a journalist to travel to Cherbourg, north of Brisbane, to interview him about bodyline. The journalist returned with a story, published by newspapers throughout Australia, in which Gilbert was quoted as saying, 'I have absolutely no objection to bowling leg-theory, and, further, I will get more wickets by doing so.' The press played up this possibility in the days that followed. An unnamed 'prominent official' of the Queensland Cricket Association was quoted as saying that unless the MCC stopped Jardine bowling bodyline Gilbert would be 'instructed' to bowl leg-theory at the Englishmen. J. S. Hutcheon, one of Queensland's two delegates to the Board of Control, was reported to have said that the Board would not interfere with any attempt by the Queenslanders to bowl leg-theory in the match against the MCC. 'That is the captain's province entirely,' Hutcheon was quoted as saying. All the indications are that Gilbert was being 'set up' by the press – that he really had no interest in bowling bodyline at the Englishmen. By all accounts, he was a shy, non-aggressive and rather guileless individual, not at all the kind of man to lead a counter-offensive against Jardine's bodyline. In the event, Gilbert bowled in completely orthodox fashion when Queensland played the MCC a week before the fourth Test. He did bowl a few very fast overs, fast enough to beat Sutcliffe several times with pace, and once, when he got Leyland to snick the ball to the wicketkeeper, Waterman, the ball was too hot for Waterman to hold and struck him in the stomach. Waterman doubled up in pain on the ground and took several minutes to recover. It is also said that Gilbert hit Jardine on the hip severely enough to bring out a livid bruise but that Jardine gave no indication he had been hurt until he returned to the dressing room and collapsed on a bench. Another story is told of a nearly identical occurrence in the fifth Test, when Jardine was hit by the Victorian fast bowler Harry Alexander, and perhaps one of the two stories deserves to be treated with circumspection. Jack Fingleton wrote in later years that Jardine had told him the remark from the crowd he most enjoyed that summer was one made while he was batting against Gilbert. A barracker called out 'Get stuck into this — — — pommy, Gilbert. It was his — — — mob that took all that land from your — — — mob.' This was in reference to Jardine's distant family connection with the Jardine brothers who occupied vast areas of North Queensland for cattle-raising.

For Australians, the question of retaliation was a vexed one. It was raised from time to time during the series, but it does not seem to have ever been considered seriously, at least by people in a position to do something about it. It might be argued, without being overly cynical, that this was because Australia did not have fast bowlers capable of bowling bodyline. Its leading fast bowler, Tim Wall, was accurate but not particularly hostile. Its most hostile fast bowler, Harry Alexander, was not noted for great accuracy. Whether this would have prevented them from bowling bodyline effectively is another matter. According to one school of thought, to which Bill O'Reilly has always belonged, bowling bodyline successfully did not require nearly as much skill as many Englishmen liked to believe. Whatever the truth of that, the fact is that Bill Woodfull would never countenance the idea of retaliation. Bill O'Reilly says this was simply a matter of principle with him. Vic Richardson is said to have admitted later that if he had been captain in 1932–33 he would have used bodyline tactics against the Englishmen, and, in fact, he did use a form of leg-theory against them when they played South Australia at the end of the tour. But, perhaps in deference to Woodfull's views, the possibility of retaliating was rarely discussed in the Australian dressing room.

Sir William McKell, later Premier of New South Wales and Governor-General of Australia, had a brief but revealing conversation with Woodfull on the subject when they sat next to each other at lunch during one of the Sydney Tests. Sir William raised the matter by saying that in his experience as a Rugby footballer the only way to counter rough tactics was to use rough tactics yourself. Whereupon Woodfull turned to him and said, 'Do you suggest we should retaliate?' When Sir William said that was exactly what he was suggesting, Woodfull dismissed the idea rather testily and would not discuss it further. Sir William says he clearly resented the suggestion even being put to him.

Fingleton and Grimmett were dropped for the fourth Test and were replaced by two left-handed batsmen, Len Darling and E. H. Bromley, the reasoning being apparently that left-handers would not be so vulnerable to a bodyline attack since Larwood would not be able to angle the ball into them. Oldfield, still not fit to play after his injury at Adelaide, was replaced behind the stumps by H. S. Love.

Woodfull won the toss and chose to bat. Bodyline never looked so ineffectual as it did on the first day of this Test. The day was hot, the wicket played easily and Larwood did not have Voce's support at the other end. Vic Richardson opened the batting with Woodfull, and for some time the Englishmen were reluctant to use bodyline against him. Larwood moved his fieldsmen into the bodyline trap in his fourth over while bowling to Woodfull, but Jardine continued to set an orthodox field for Richardson. Perhaps this was because Jardine feared Richardson's strength on the on-side; more probably, it was because he simply believed Larwood had a better chance of getting Richardson out by conventional means on this particular wicket. In any case, bodyline was used against Richardson, too, later in the pre-lunch session. When the score passed 100 without the fall of a wicket, however, Jardine decided to abandon the bodyline field altogether and shifted his men back to the off-side, a move which was greeted, we are told, by 'an outburst of cheering mingled with derisive shouts' from the crowd. Tom Goodman wrote in the paper next day, 'For the first time the leg-theory attack had been mastered.'

Richardson was brilliantly stumped by Ames off Hammond's bowling when he was 83 and the total was 133, easily the highest opening partnership by the Australians in the series. Bradman came in next, and at once Jardine brought Larwood back into the attack and set a bodyline field. It was not the customary leg-theory field, however. There were only three short-legs, one or two fewer than usual, but on the other hand Jardine placed three men in the deep on the leg-side, no doubt expecting Bradman to adopt the same adventurous approach that he had at Adelaide and perhaps try to hook the bouncers. In fact, Bradman began shakily, and continued to play shakily until the tea adjournment, but after that he found touch. The first ball he faced after tea, from Larwood, was driven with great power to the mid-off boundary. He scored freely off all the English bowlers in this final session, including Larwood, and was 71 not out at stumps. Ponsford was the other overnight batsman, and the score was 3 for 251.

Australia had not been in such a strong position so early before, and much was expected of the Australian batsmen on the second day. At worst, Bradman could be counted on to score the 29 runs he needed for his century. Instead, it proved to be for Australia a day of terrible disappointment. The last seven wickets fell for only 89 runs. Larwood bowled with much more fire

than on the previous day, and from his very first over
he bowled to a bodyline field. Bradman was apparently
uncomfortable against him. He repeatedly ducked or
pulled away from lifting deliveries, and in Larwood's
third over, the sixth of the morning, he drew back to
cut a ball pitched on the leg stump, but seemed to be
beaten by the pace of it and was bowled. His 76 runs
had included 11 fours and had taken 156 minutes. A
record crowd for Brisbane of 28,572 had come to see
Bradman bat, and his early dismissal must have been a
sharp disappointment for them.

Fielding in the heat on the first day of the Test,
Eddie Paynter began to feel unwell and at the end of
the day's play was diagnosed as suffering from tonsilitis
and slight sun-stroke. When his condition had not
improved by the following day, Saturday, it was
decided to move him from the team's hotel into a
private hospital. He was still ill on Sunday morning,
and when Warner told Jardine then that it was doubtful
if Paynter would be able to bat on Monday Jardine
said, 'What about those fellows who marched to Kan-
dahar with the fever on them?' – a remark which, said
Warner, 'delighted me and was typical of our captain's
grit and determination'.

At that stage, neither Jardine nor Warner would
have seen any pressing need for Paynter to bat anyway.
In reply to Australia's first innings total of 340, England
was no wicket for 99 at stumps on Saturday. But on
Monday the English innings began to collapse. Five
wickets fell, three of them to O'Reilly, before the
score reached 200. Paynter was now badly needed at
the crease, and at some time in the afternoon he was
extricated from his hospital bed and brought to the
English dressing room to pad up.

There are conflicting accounts of how this happened.

Larwood wrote that Bill Voce was responsible for getting Paynter to the ground. He said Voce had been sitting by Paynter's bed in the hospital, keeping him company, when he learned of the fall of wickets and told Paynter about it. Paynter insisted on getting up, Larwood said, and Voce took him in a car to the ground. Bill Ferguson said it was Jardine's idea to get Paynter out of hospital, and it seems this is Bob Wyatt's belief, too. Ferguson wrote, 'He [Jardine] decided that Paynter was going to bat, even if he had to get an ambulance to transport Eddie to the ground. Accordingly, Bill Voce was delegated to smuggle Eddie Paynter's clothes into the hospital and – a much more difficult task – get Eddie out of the place to report for batting duty.' Larwood says Paynter looked white and ill when he came in, sixth wicket down, late in the day, and he still had the shakes. Doses of brandy and eggs were sent out to him to help keep him going, and Paynter was still there at stumps on 24. He spent that night back in his hospital bed, but returned to the crease next day and went on to make 83. Largely because of him, the Englishmen were able to take their score to 356, 16 ahead of Australia. Warner said he never saw a grander example of grit and guts on a cricket field than Paynter's at Brisbane. It was certainly a very brave innings, yet in a sense Paynter did have heroism thrust upon him by his captain.

The Australians did not offer so much resistance in their second innings as in their first. Woodfull and Richardson put on 46 for the first wicket, but thereafter there was a steady turnover of batsmen at the crease. Bradman made 24, and again it was Larwood who took his wicket. Bradman batted aggressively, taking 12 off one over from Larwood. Twice, off consecutive balls, he stepped back in his accustomed fashion and cut short-pitched balls from Larwood to the point boundary. Tommy Mitchell was moved to point to cut off the shot, and when in Larwood's next over Bradman stepped back again to cut he hit a catch straight to him. Australia was all out in its second innings for 175, which meant England needed only 160 runs for victory. It lost only four wickets in making them, and it was probably appropriate that a match which Pelham Warner later referred to as 'Paynter's match' should have been brought to an end by Paynter himself, hitting a six off McCabe to score the winning runs.

On the second-last day of the Test, cricket suffered a distressing loss when Archie Jackson, the young Sydney batsman, died in a Brisbane hospital. There is every chance that Jackson would have been playing in the Tests of 1932–33 if he had not contracted tuberculosis and been forced out of big cricket at the end of 1931. Jackson had risen to prominence about the same time as Bradman, and for a time some commentators were inclined to rate his prospects as highly as Bradman's. He was a fluent, stylish batsman, and he made a tremendous impression on English and Australian observers alike when he scored a brilliant 164 in his first Test in 1928–29. But whereas Bradman's career soared to amazing heights in 1930, Jackson's faltered. He soon ceased to be considered a rival to Bradman, and his place in the Australian team was thereafter in doubt.

It had been speculated that Jackson may have suffered from the effects of tuberculosis as early as 1929, which would help to explain his loss of form. The disease was diagnosed at the end of 1931, and Jackson spent the winter of 1932 resting and recovering his health in the Blue Mountains. He moved to Brisbane in September that year, ostensibly for the good of his health, but the real reason, probably, was that he wanted to be near his girlfriend, who lived there. Jackson was advised by his doctor to return to the Blue Mountains before the summer and on no account to play cricket, but he disregarded the advice entirely. He stayed in Brisbane and he played club cricket regularly, actually with wonderful success. His health broke down, as the doctor warned it would, at the end of January 1933, and he was admitted to a private hospital, where he died on 15 February, aged twenty-three. Several newspaper articles had appeared under Jackson's name in the preceding weeks which were critical of the Australian batsmen's failures against bodyline, although Jackson was not necessarily the author of them. Still, he must have had some sympathy for the English cause. During the third Test he sent Larwood a telegram congratulating him on his 'magnificent' bowling and wishing him luck in future matches. Jackson's body was returned to Sydney on the same train which brought the Australian cricketers back from the Test, and six Australian players, Woodfull, Richardson, Bradman, McCabe, Oldfield and Ponsford, were pallbearers at his funeral.

England's win in the fourth Test meant that Douglas Jardine had accomplished what he set out to do – he had recovered the Ashes. England's lead in the series was now an unbeatable 3 to 1. It remained to be seen whether victory had softened him, and whether he might now decide to spare the Australian batsmen the full rigours of bodyline bowling in the final Test at Sydney.

13

The Last Act

The attendance on the first day of the fifth Test in Sydney, 26,143, was small compared with the attendance there on the same day of the first Test, 58,058, but it was big enough to show there was still interest in the cricket, even though the Ashes had been decided. It is probable that by now the spectacle of bodyline in action – of Larwood bowling very fast and short, of the English fieldsmen crouching behind the batsman like predators, of the Australians ducking and weaving to avoid being hit – had come to hold its own grim fascination for Australian spectators. We have no way of confirming this, but it is likely that bodyline attracted many people to the grounds that summer who did not ordinarily go to the cricket but who were curious to see what all the fuss was about. Bradman's continuing duels with Larwood must also have held a special fascination for the crowds, although the crowds were not so optimistic about the outcome as they were to begin with. If what the men in the press box were writing was any indication of what people at large were thinking, there was by now general resignation to the idea that Jardine's bodyline could not be overcome, even by Bradman. It is not hard to detect the growing acceptance of this in the press reports of the play during the series. By the end of the series cricket writers had ceased to express amazement at Bradman's failure to make big scores as they had at the start.

Again the Australian selectors tinkered with the batting line-up. Ponsford, who made 19 and 0 in

Brisbane, was dropped for the second time in the series and was replaced, not by Fingleton as some might have expected, but by Leo O'Brien, who had already played in one Test, the second, and failed. Bromley was replaced by P. K. Lee, an all-rounder, Oldfield resumed his place at the expense of Love, and Harry Alexander was brought in in place of Wall, who was injured. The English needed to make only one change: Voce back, Mitchell out.

Jardine may have been tempted, now that the Ashes had been won, to give Maurice Tate a game, but if so the temptation was resisted. Tate had the unhappiest tour of all the Englishmen. He was regarded as one of the world's best bowlers in the 1920s, but in 1932–33 his medium-pace, full-length bowling had no place in Jardine's plans, and he was left on the sidelines for all the important matches. Even if you follow the story of the tour closely, you keep forgetting Tate was there. The truth was that Jardine was intent on pressing home the advantage bodyline gave him to the bitter end. There was to be no mercy for the vanquished. He was determined to apply his bodyline methods as rigorously as ever, and in a sense he really couldn't afford not to. If he abandoned his leg-theory in the fifth Test, it would have been seen by some as an admission by him that there was something undesirable about it, after all. And if he did abandon it and Australia won the Test, it would have been used as proof for ever after that the Englishmen could not have won the Ashes by conventional means. In the event, he moved his fieldsmen into the bodyline cordon as early as Voce's third over, the sixth over of the match.

As at Brisbane, Australia ended the first day on a fairly high note, 5 for 196. Bradman had come and gone for 48, another brief, brilliant innings which, as

Eric Barbour said in the paper next day, violated all the conventions. He made his 48 runs in 71 minutes, during which time his partner, Woodfull, scored only 16. Against Larwood, he variously ducked, dodged and stepped back to hit to the off. When Allen was brought into the attack he attacked him so savagely that Allen's first two overs cost 21 runs. Larwood got him in the end, as he had several times got Ponsford, by bowling him behind his legs as he stepped inside the line of the ball to glance. McCabe batted steadily for 73, his highest score since the first Test, but the mainstay of the innings was Darling who went on next day to make 85. While he was batting on the first day, drinks were brought out for the English fieldsmen, and Jardine was thoughtful enough to bring a drink over to him. Immediately, a barracker yelled out, 'Be very careful, O'Brien – taste it before you drink it.' Even Jardine, we are told, could scarce forbear to smile.

Australia made 435 in its first innings, by a long way its highest total of the series, but it proved to be not high enough. England's reply was 19 runs better, 454, and for that Hammond, who made 101, and Larwood, 98, could take most of the credit. Larwood's innings was an extraordinary one. In the earlier Tests he had never batted higher than number nine, and sometimes as low as eleven. He went in at number four here as a nightwatchman, and on the following day, with nothing to lose, he threw his bat at everything within reach. His score increased at a rate which must have alarmed the Australian captain, Woodfull, until, at 84, he faced a new over from Lee.

Larwood got the first ball away to square leg for two, drove the second towards the Randwick-end sight-board for six, mishit the third through gully for two and pulled the fourth for four. Suddenly, he was on

98, only a stroke away from his century. Perhaps the imminence of the triumph made him tense up, for off the next ball he spooned a catch to mid-on, where it was accepted by Bert Ironmonger, widely reckoned to be one of the worst fieldsmen in the game. There was loud applause as Larwood walked back to the pavilion. At first he thought the crowd was applauding Lee and Ironmonger for getting him out, but by the time he arrived at the gate he realized the applause was actually for his marvellous innings.

Australia made only 182 in its second innings, thereby following the pattern of second-innings failures which began in the first Test. In each of the five Tests Australia made many fewer runs in its second innings than in its first. Its first-innings totals were 360, 228, 222, 340 and 435. Its second-innings totals were 164, 191, 193, 175 and 182. Thus, Australia never made less than 222 in its first innings, it never made more than 193 in its second. In aggregate, its first innings were 75 per cent higher than its second innings. This would be easy enough to understand if Verity had taken plenty of second-innings wickets on wearing pitches, but in fact he did this only once, in the fifth Test. No other explanation comes readily to mind, except perhaps this one: that bodyline somehow weakened the moral resistance of the Australian batsmen in the course of each Test, with the result that they were not so well equipped, mentally, to withstand the barrage in the second innings as in the first. In other words, they were softened up in the first round for a quick knock-out in the second. This is all highly suppositional, of course, yet the fact remains that apart from Bradman, who did it several times, and Woodfull, who did it twice, not one Australian batsman managed to improve his first-innings score appreciably in the second innings.

Bradman's final joust with bodyline was the most exciting of the series. He made 71 in 97 minutes in Australia's second innings, and by all accounts he came closer to mastering bodyline with his planned unorthodoxy in this innings than in any other. Larwood set his usual bodyline field for Bradman to begin with, but Bradman forced Jardine to change it repeatedly, and later Larwood had two men stationed in the gully area. Jack Fingleton did not play in this match, of course, but we may be sure he watched every ball of it, and later he wrote this vivid account of Bradman's innings:

'When Larwood was still two or three yards from delivering the ball, Bradman was on the move. First he went to the off, then to the leg. Bradman made 71 and barely a stroke he made was known to the text book. It was the riskiest and most thrilling batting imaginable . . . Bradman's stumps were left open not once but a dozen times. An ordinary straight ball from Larwood would have been sufficient then to end Bradman's innings, but it really seemed that the stumps were of minor concern to both Bradman and Larwood. It seemed that Larwood was anxious to claim a hit on Bradman in this final Test – a thing the Englishman had not done previously. And Bradman seemed just as determined Larwood shouldn't.'

Pelham Warner wrote: 'Bradman was in his most dominating mood and made the most amazing strokes off Larwood and Voce, stepping away from his wicket and forcing the ball on the off. His first four was a sort of smash which you see at lawn tennis.' Another eye-witness, C. R. Ashford, provides this description of that stroke:

'The first ball Bradman received from Larwood was a bumper. Bradman used his bat like a tennis racquet, and the ball bounded on the first bounce on to the sightboard in front of the old Northern Stand – over Larwood's head! The only fieldsmen on the off were Voce at third man and Leyland two-thirds of the way to the fence at extra cover.'

During this innings Larwood finally scored the hit on Bradman which Fingleton claimed he was seeking. A short, rising ball struck Bradman high on the left arm, and, although he continued batting almost immediately, the arm was too sore to allow him to field on the following day, and apparently for the only time in his first-class career Bradman carried the drinks. (He did not carry them when he was twelfth man in the second Test in 1928–29; he fielded for the whole of that match in place of Ponsford, who had had his thumb broken by Larwood.) Jardine wrote that Bradman was hit by Larwood when he tried to cut a ball six to nine inches outside the leg stump. As in Adelaide, Bradman lost his wicket unexpectedly to Verity, hitting over a ball which went on to bowl him. When he left the field, Larwood left with him, limping on an injured left foot. That glory of Larwood's bowling action, the great thrust upwards and forwards of his left leg, seemed to have been the cause of the injury. Larwood had brought his left foot down so hard and so often that summer that the very structure of it was under strain, and in this second innings of the last Test the foot finally gave way. Although Larwood was not aware of it at the time, a small bone in the foot had been fractured.

The story has often been told of how Jardine insisted on Larwood remaining on the field until Bradman was out, apparently in the belief that his very presence would keep Bradman under psychological pressure. In

The Larwood Story, Larwood says that when he asked
to go off Jardine said to him, 'You can't go off
while this little bastard's in.' Without questioning the
accuracy of this story, it may be noted for the record
that Larwood bowled to Bradman until almost the very
end of his innings. In fact, Bradman raised his score to
71 by off-driving Larwood for three. It was off the
second ball of the very next over that Bradman tried
to drive Verity, hit over it and was bowled. Thus,
Bradman survived only one delivery after Larwood
bowled his last ball of the series. In view of Jardine's
insistence that he should stay on the field and in view
of the discomfort the foot must have been causing, it
was fortunate for Larwood that Bradman got out as
quickly as he did.

There was one last, unpleasant incident to be recorded before it all came to an end. Late that same
day, when Jardine and Wyatt began England's second
innings, the English captain complained several times
to the umpire that the Australian fast bowler Alexander was running on the pitch in his follow-through.
This irritated the crowd, which loudly hooted Jardine,
and it also irritated Alexander, who was an aggressive
and genuinely fast bowler. Alexander proceeded to
bowl at Jardine in a most hostile fashion, and in his
fourth over he hit him hard in the left side. The *Sydney
Morning Herald* described it as a 'sickening blow'.
Immediately there was a roar of approval from the
crowd, followed by sustained applause for Alexander.
It was probably the most reprehensible thing Australian barrackers did all summer, and it is a certainty that
Jardine carried home the memory of it.

England lost only two wickets next day while making
the 164 it needed for victory. Hammond scored the
winning runs by off-driving Lee deep into the Sheridan

Stand for six. Afterwards, in the Australian dressing room, Vic Richardson called the players together, spoke a few words in praise of Woodfull's captaincy and led the team in giving him three rousing cheers. Woodfull went across to the English dressing room and congratulated Jardine. But there were no official speeches.

The Englishmen played two more matches, against Victoria and South Australia, to complete the tour, and in the latter match, their last in Australia, the South Australian captain, Vic Richardson, used a form of bodyline against them. He placed five fieldsmen on the leg-side and had his pace bowlers, Tobin and Williams, bounce the ball at the English batsmen. Richardson must have done this as merely a parting gesture, for neither of his bowlers was fast enough to cause the Englishmen serious alarm, and in any case his 'bodyline' was unsuccessful. But the chairman of the Board of Control, Dr Robertson, was not amused. It seems he feared Richardson's action might compromise the Board in its dealings with the MCC. In a letter to Jeanes, the secretary of the South Australian Cricket Association, he said, 'To think your captain resorted to it after your association had placed on record a minute protesting against it appears to me an indication of his irresponsibility in such a crisis as is facing us at the moment. It beats my comprehension.' Jeanes replied with a report on the incident:

'It cannot be denied that there was sufficient departure from orthodox methods to give some ground for the exaggerated versions which have been published. Neither were the bowlers Tobin and Williams fast enough to cause fear of injury. Those bowlers, however, particularly Williams, bowled a very big proportion of bumpers and kept the batsman almost continually ducking.'

The Englishmen made a parting gesture of their own in this match. When Jardine led his players on to the field, five of the professionals – Ames, Mitchell, Leyland, Paynter and Voce – were seen to be wearing Harlequin caps. Jardine, on the other hand, wore a blue English cap.

They had got back at the barrackers in the end.

14

A Reassessment

The difficulty of trying to assess today the effectiveness of Jardine's bodyline is that there is nothing else in cricket it can be measured against. Bodyline proper was bowled for only one season and by only one team, so it has to be studied and evaluated more or less in isolation. It is true the West Indians did try to bowl something similar against England in 1933, but it is generally accepted that the West Indians' bodyline was a pretty poor imitation of the real thing. Thus, we have no way of telling how proficient Larwood and Voce really were at bowling bodyline, because we cannot compare their performance (Larwood 33 wickets in five Tests, Voce 15 in four) with the performance of any of the other great fast-bowling pairs – say, McDonald and Gregory, or Lindwall and Miller, or Tyson and Statham. Nor do we have any reliable way of telling how proficient the Australian batsmen were at dealing with it. It was the opinion of Jardine and perhaps some of the other Englishmen that the Australians handled bodyline badly. 'Macartney, Ryder and Bardsley, to take at random only three names from recent cricket history, would, in my opinion, have made very short work of leg-theory,' Jardine wrote. In fact, it is impossible to say how Macartney and Bardsley, or Barnes and Morris, or Simpson and Lawry, or Greg and Ian Chappell would have fared against bodyline, none of them faced anything that closely resembled it, which is not to say Macartney and Bardsley did not on occasions face leg-theory.

Yet there is one player whose uniqueness entitles us to use him as a benchmark – Don Bradman. Bradman's performances so far outstripped those of all other batsmen in the history of the game, before and since, that it can be argued that if he could not succeed against bodyline, nobody could. Bradman did succeed against bodyline to this extent: his average for the series, 56.57, was not only higher than any other Australian batsman's by a long way, but it was higher than the average of any of the English batsmen, too, apart from Paynter, who played in only three Tests and was not out twice. On the other hand, the statistics show that Bradman fared worse against bodyline, as measured by his own standards, than did all the other leading Australian batsmen as measured by theirs, with the exception of Ponsford and, if you wished to include him, Kippax. The following are the batting averages of leading Australian players in 1932–33 expressed as a proportion of their career averages against England: Bradman 63.0 per cent, Woodfull 76.9 per cent, Ponsford 49.8 per cent, McCabe 88.6 per cent, Fingleton 78.2 per cent. This might be taken to mean that Bradman performed at 63 per cent of capacity against bodyline, Woodfull at 77 per cent, Ponsford 50 per cent, McCabe 89 per cent and Fingleton 78 per cent, although this would be making more of the statistics than we are probably entitled to do, and in any case we would not be taking into account the fact that some batsmen had more bodyline bowled at them than others. It is possible to demonstrate statistically that Jardine concentrated his bodyline attack on Bradman more than on any other Australian. Larwood bowled 28.5 per cent of the balls which Bradman faced in the series. For other batsmen the equivalent percentages were: Woodfull 28.0, Fingleton 27.5, Ponsford 23.9,

McCabe 24.0 and Richardson 18.8. This shows that Jardine had Larwood bowling more often to Bradman than to any other batsman. Furthermore, there is no doubt that Larwood bowled to a bodyline field – that is, bowled bodyline – more persistently to Bradman than to any other batsman. To Woodfull and Fingleton, for instance, he often bowled to an off-side field at the start of an innings, but time and time again we read that he moved his field into the bodyline format as soon as Bradman came to the crease.

It is possible to say this much at least: Bradman did not perform well enough, for Bradman, in 1932–33 to convince everyone that the unorthodox methods he employed to try to counter bodyline were necessarily the best methods, even for him. Jardine (who, admittedly, was not an unbiased critic) argued later that Bradman would have done better to try to counter bodyline with orthodox methods, as he did when he scored a century in the second Test. 'Why he ever deserted such methods will always remain a mystery to me,' Jardine wrote. But Jardine did not have to face bodyline – at least the kind of bodyline Bradman had to face – and there is no reason he or anyone else should have been a better judge than Bradman of Bradman's own capabilities.

There is one other factor to consider, which does not seem to have been considered elsewhere, and that is the factor of luck. It is impossible to study the newspaper accounts of Bradman's sorties against bodyline and not conclude that the Englishmen were really very fortunate to get him out as cheaply as they did. In his last five Test innings Bradman scored 66, 76, 24, 48 and 71, and in each of these innings he gave promise of cutting loose against Larwood. In several of them, indeed, he did cut loose, and a quick century or double century was in the offing. If luck had run more in his direction and if, in particular, he had not rather rashly lost his wicket twice to Verity when he had overcome the might of Larwood, the double-century may have eventuated. It is worth noting how rapidly Bradman scored in the bodyline Tests. Against all bowlers he scored at the rate of 4.5 runs for each six balls faced and against Larwood he scored at a slightly faster rate, 4.6 runs for each six balls faced. This, it may be noted, is the average rate at which a team needs to score to make 230 in a one-day, 50-over-a-side match, a rate which international sides are not often able to achieve. Bradman's speed of scoring seems all the more remarkable when it is remembered that in four of his eight Test innings in the bodyline series he came to the wicket after one of the openers had scored a duck – in other words, he was a de facto opener. The bowler who suffered most from Bradman's bat in the Tests was Allen, the one fast bowler who never bowled bodyline. Bradman scored off him at the amazing rate of 5.0 runs for each six balls faced, and Allen did not once take his wicket. By comparison with these figures, McCabe's rate of scoring in his hectic innings of 187 not out in the first Test was 4.8 runs for each six balls faced, which is only slightly higher than Bradman's rate over the whole series. John Arlott remembers a conversation he had with Jardine after the war, in which Jardine recalled the Englishmen's victory in 1932–33. 'You know, we nearly didn't do it,' Jardine said. 'The little man was bloody good.'

Bradman scored faster off Allen than off Larwood, and he scored faster off Hammond (4.6 runs for each six balls faced) than off Voce (3.9). It is wrong, therefore, to imagine he made a frantic assault upon the bodyline bowlers in particular that summer, for he actually scored faster on the whole off those who bowled to a conventional off-side field. The tempo of his batting was stepped up generally. It seemed as if he were intent on making as many runs as he could, while he could, and the reason for that, probably, was that he gave himself little chance of surviving long against the bodyline attack, given the high-risk nature of the tactics he was using to counter it. In an interview on ABC radio in the mid-1970s, Sir Donald said, 'The man never lived who could consistently and successfully combat the 1932–33 bodyline attack.' It seems this was a view shared by the other Australian batsmen. Bill Ponsford still holds it today. 'I still don't think anybody in the world could have dealt with it,' he says. It is possible, perhaps probable, that Bradman decided there was no satisfactory answer to bodyline in the course of the series. Several English observers detected a certain fatalism in his approach, as if he were resolved to go down fighting and yet was resigned to going down nevertheless. It may be too, that Bradman's refusal to use conventional methods against bodyline was itself a gesture of condemnation. Conversely it may have seemed to Bradman that to play conventionally would have been to accept bodyline as a legitimate form of attack.

Jack Hobbs made the following statement to a reporter just before he left Australia:

'The Australian batsmen had my sympathy in playing leg-theory. It is all very well to talk, but the man at the wicket has much less time to think than the man in the grandstand. Bradman would have none of it. I thought he gave up a little early. He took the view that he was not going to be hit and acted accordingly. He made some extraordinary strokes, and I think he has more strokes now than when he visited England.'

Bill Bowes still believes Bradman might have searched longer for a way to overcome bodyline. 'There may not have been an answer to it,' he says, 'but if there was Bradman was the one man who could have come up with it. But he damned it as soon as he saw it. I will always be sorry he did not really give it a go.' It is true that Bradman damned bodyline as soon as he saw it, and in doing so he was a step ahead of one or two Board of Control members who were not prepared to listen when Bradman and others expressed concern about the Englishmen's tactics as soon as they were used. It is also true that in the fifty-odd years since the bodyline Tests, nobody has thought of a better way to play bodyline than Bradman's.

Gubby Allen says that he and some of the other Englishmen believed at the time that the Australians would have been wise to take guard outside the leg stump. Their reasoning was that a batsman taking normal guard had two things to worry about when Larwood or Voce bounced a ball in his direction: would it hit him or would it hit the stumps? If he took guard outside the leg stump he had only one thing to worry about: getting out of its way. At least one Australian batsman, Vic Richardson, did try doing this, and Richardson averaged only 27.9 in the Tests and might have been dropped if there had been a sixth Test played. Allen makes one other interesting comment on the matter. He says bodyline was more difficult to handle in 1932–33 than it might have been at any other time or place, because of the exceptional variation in bounce of the Australian pitches that season. Allen says:

'Harold would rush in, drop one a bit short and it would come through, say, shoulder high. The next one would drop in exactly the same spot and come through hip high. The number of times I saw that happen . . . Now, the Australians used to go and duck; there are millions of pictures of them doing it, ducking and getting hit. Or if a ball came through hip high they would decide to stand up and play the next one, and it would come through shoulder high. It made it very, very difficult. I think bodyline would have succeeded in any case, but it would never have had anything like the success and, indeed, the number of people being hit if it had not been for this uneven bounce.'

The depressant effect which bodyline had on the Australians' scoring in 1932–33 had several curious features. We have already seen how in every Test bodyline seemed to make a greater impact in the second innings than in the first. It was also strangely successful in pegging back the Australian batsmen whenever they threatened to go on to make a large score. Attention has been drawn to the fact that Bradman scored in the 60s and 70s three times in the last three Tests without being able to advance to 100 and beyond, as in ordinary circumstances he would have been expected to do. Other Australians were contained in the same way. Four of them managed to progress as far as the 80s (Fingleton 83, Richardson 83, Darling 85 and Ponsford 85) and Woodfull three times progressed beyond 60 (to 73 not out, 67 and 67), but they were able to go no further. This may have been simply a statistical oddity, but it is reasonable to speculate that the special nature of the English attack had something to do with it. Perhaps it was, again, the wearing effect which bodyline seemed to have on batsmen which was responsible. It may be that by the time an Australian made 70 or 80 against the England attack of 1932–33 he did not feel, as a batsman would normally feel, settled and confident, but felt jaded and fatigued, in mind as well as body. Jack Fingleton certainly felt this way when he made a century against Voce's bodyline for New South Wales.

In *Cricket Crisis*, Jack Fingleton said that after the bodyline experience Bradman never regained his poise of 1930. He did have a marvellous season in Sheffield Shield cricket in the following summer, 1933–34, averaging 132.44 at his eleven visits to the crease, yet when he failed in the first three Tests of the 1934 series in England many were convinced he was still suffering from the after-effects of bodyline. However that may be, he did score a triple-century in the fourth Test and a double-century in the fifth, and even if in the years that followed he did not score with quite the prolificacy of 1930, he did score at a rate very close to it. When nearly all Jardine's players were retired or dead, Bradman was still making Test double-centuries. It is a fact, too, that Bradman's relative failures against bodyline did not affect his standing with the Australian public. He was as big a star at the end of the 1932–33 season as he was at the beginning. As Australians saw it, Bradman had been prevented from making his usual big scores by unfair means, and for that reason his failure to make those scores did not really count.

15

Repercussions

When Gubby Allen met the secretary of the MCC, Billy Findlay, at Lord's after his return to England, Findlay said to him, 'What a terrible time you must have had in Australia . . . I refuse to believe that any Englishman ever bowled at a batsman.' Allen replied, 'The sooner you try to find out what's been going on, the better for cricket.' As a result of that exchange, Allen and Findlay did not speak to each other for two years. The kind of ignorance Allen encountered here was to bedevil dealings between the Board of Control and the MCC over the bodyline issue for months to come. The two bodies believed they were talking about the same thing, but they were really talking about two different things – the tactics which the Board knew Jardine to have used and the tactics the MCC understood him to have used. The chief cause of the discrepancy, it seems, was the inadequate reporting of the Tests by the small English press contingent. At the time, the Board's representative in England was a former captain of Queensland, Dr Robert Macdonald, and in June 1933, he told the Board's secretary, Jeanes, in a letter, 'The whole press here throughout the controversy have set themselves to advocate England's case, even to the extent of censoring news from Australia.' For instance, Macdonald said, it had not been reported in England that Jardine had moved his bodyline field into position after Woodfull was hit in Adelaide. 'Even Mr Findlay was not aware of it a month ago when I described it to him,' Macdonald

said. 'If that incident at Adelaide had been published
here, Jardine's mentality and ruthlessness would have
been markedly revealed to the English people. The
veil of silence was drawn over it by the press.'

There is no doubt that the Fleet Street newspapers
did adopt a strong pro-Jardine stance and, moreover,
that they were inclined to treat the Australian complaints about bodyline with some contempt and even
to question the courage of the Australian batsmen.
Australians were frequently described as 'squealers'
and one newspaper published a verse in which reference was made to 'a whining Digger funking knocks'.
In the Australian Cricket Board's archives there is a
letter written in July 1933 by an unnamed Australian
war widow living at Grayshott in Surrey, in which she
appeals to the Board of Control to cancel all further
matches against England until bodyline was prohibited.
'It is not only the articles that appear in the daily press
that are so insulting,' she said, 'but everywhere one
goes one hears insulting remarks about the attitude of
the different players and the cowardice of Woodfull,
Bradman and Oldfield and the sarcasm about the
flinching of the two former batsmen when Larwood is
bowling.'

Lloyd Dumas, the Adelaide newspaper editor who,
as we have seen, took part in a peace-making initiative
immediately after the Adelaide Test, had a special
concern about the attitude of the English newspapers,
whose comments about the bodyline issue were being
quoted at length in the Australian press. Dumas
believed the attitude of the British press was unfair to
Australians, but, quite apart from that, he was alarmed
by the bitterness the English comments were causing
in Australia. Accordingly, he wrote to the editors of
The Times, Daily Telegraph, Manchester *Guardian,*

Morning Post, News Chronicle and the *Daily Mail*, appealing to them to tone down their anti-Australian comments and to present the Australian side of the case if they could. He also wrote to the editors of all Australian metropolitan newspapers, beseeching them to use their influence to try to restore peace to the cricket world. Dumas believed his efforts were generally successful. He wrote, 'When I visited London in 1935, I was entertained at lunch at *The Times*. and, in a jocular way, was accused of being a "squealer". The memory still lingered, but there was no more sting in it.'

After the dispute about bodyline bowling blew up at the Adelaide Test, the Board of Control appointed a committee to report on ways of eliminating bodyline from Australian cricket. The committee consisted of Woodfull and Richardson, a Queensland Board delegate, J. T. Hartigan, and the pre-war Australian captain, Monty Noble. In April 1933, the committee recommended the creation of a new cricket law, empowering umpires to no-ball fast bowlers who bowled a ball judged to be intimidatory in intent and to suspend them from bowling for the rest of the innings if they repeated the offence. The recommendation was cabled to the MCC on 28 April. The MCC sent a lengthy reply on 12 June, which repudiated again the suggestion that Jardine's fast bowlers bowled at the batsmen, rejected the proposed law as unworkable and finally complained about the barracking the English players had been subjected to in Australia.

This amounted to a renewal of hostilities between the Board and MCC, and the 1934 tour of England was placed in doubt again. What the Board really wanted was an assurance that bodyline would not be used against the Australians in England, and the MCC clearly was in no mood to give it. About this time, Dr Macdonald, who lived at Leicester, began lobbying at Lord's on behalf of the Board. Several reports he sent to the Board in the second half of 1933, written in his own rather shaky hand, are preserved in the Australian Cricket Board's archives. They reveal how extraordinarily delicate negotiations between the two cricket authorities were. On 1 August, he wrote that he had met several members of the MCC Committee, Lord Hailsham, Lord Hawke, Sir Stanley Jackson and Lord Lewisham, who suggested that the whole matter be deferred until the Australians arrived in 1934. Macdonald replied this would be unacceptable, because if bodyline was to be permitted in 1934 the Australians would want to include four fast bowlers in their team to provide a 'shock attack' of their own. At this, Lord Hawke remarked, 'Reprisals, by God!' Dr Macdonald replied, 'No, I would call it reciprocity.' Having thus tested the temper of the most influential men in the MCC, Macdonald proceeded to give the Board a little lecture in diplomacy. He wrote:

'I have found it expedient in my conversations with the MCC not to use it (the word "bodyline"), as they take great exception to it. Personally I recognize its exact and very fitting nomenclature, but it will be diplomatic and expedient on our part to avoid using it in any future communications with the MCC . . . I have always referred to it as "that type of bowling in Australia to which exception was taken by Australia." I think it would be safer for you to use that description of it when you cable the MCC. If we used the term Bodyline it would arouse resentment here; if we used the term leg-theory (the MCC appellation) it would to our Australian minds not be a true definition of Jardine's methods. I would advise you when cabling to the MCC to use very friendly language, for at this particular moment it will materially help our cause . . . Only tact and diplomacy are now needed to clinch and drive home our position.'

Macdonald went so far as to suggest that the Board should not say to the MCC, 'Will you guarantee' there would be no bodyline used in 1934, but should instead say, 'We request your assurance' it would not be used. 'I know from experience how sensitive they are to the way in which they are approached,' he said.

During the second half of 1933, it seems that members of the MCC Committee finally swung around to the view that Jardine's leg-theory was bad for the game and that something needed to be done, as the Australians were requesting, to make sure it was not employed in 1934. Perhaps this was because of the sheer weight of evidence against bodyline which had been accumulated at Lord's during the year. Perhaps the MCC was influenced, too, by further representations from the Secretary for the Dominions, Jimmy Thomas. In June 1933, the Governor of South Australia, Sir Alexander Hore-Ruthven, approached Thomas again, this time by letter from Adelaide, putting to him the Australian side of the dispute and informing him of the depth of feeling about the issue in Australia. 'That feeling rankles even to the extent of reluctance to buy English goods, which business men inform me is going on to a certain extent in this city today,' he said, which no doubt surprised Thomas as much as it surprises us when we read it today. E. W. Swanton, who reproduced Hore-Ruthven's letter in his book, *Follow On*, wrote that Thomas was sure to have passed on the contents of it to his Cabinet colleague, Lord Hailsham, the MCC's president. But it was not easy for the people at Lord's to admit that the Board's case did, after all, have some justice. They had defended Jardine so trenchantly until then that to do so would have required them to make a most humbling retraction, and even if they were prepared to endure that, they could not rightly expect Jardine to endure it, too. In *Follow On*, Swanton refers to a letter in which Lord Hawke was quoted as saying that the real problem was how to prevent bodyline recurring 'without letting down Douglas Jardine too badly'. In particular, the MCC could not agree to ban bodyline in 1934 without, by implication, condemning Jardine for using it in 1932–33. The problem would be solved only if the Australians were prepared to accept a tacit undertaking from the MCC that bodyline would not be bowled at them in England, instead of insisting on some formal pronouncement by the MCC to that effect.

In the light of all this, it is fascinating to study the cables exchanged by the Board and the MCC in the last few months of 1933. On 22 September, the Board sent a cable in which it reiterated its view that 'the type of bowling to which exception was taken in Australia' (the formula of words suggested by Mr Macdonald) was not in the best interests of the game. It therefore asked, 'May we assume that you concur in this point of view and that the teams may thus take the field in 1934 with that knowledge?' The MCC replied on 9 October. It agreed that any kind of bowling which amounted to a direct attack on the batsman would be against the spirit of the game, and added, 'Your team can certainly take the field with the knowledge and with the full assurance that cricket will be played here in the same spirit as in the past.' This was as close as it was possible for the MCC to go to giving the Australians the assurance they wanted without disowning Jardine, but the Australians were still not satisfied. On 16 November the Board sent the following cable to Lord's: 'We appreciate the terms of your cablegram of 9 October and assume that such cable is intended to give the assurance asked for in our cablegram of 22 September. It is on this understanding that we are sending a team in 1934.' The Board was using a sharp tactic here. In effect, the Board was saying that it believed it had detected an assurance about bodyline between the lines of the MCC's cable, but it wanted the MCC to confirm that the assurance had really been there. The MCC, however, felt it had gone as far as it could go. In a reply on 12 December, it said, 'You must please accept our cable of 9 October, which speaks for itself, as final. We cannot go beyond the assurance therein given.' The MCC wanted the issue settled once and for all, and now, for the first time, it put a time limit on the negotiations. It asked the Board to let it know by the end of the year whether or not it was sending a team.

By this time the Board of Control had acquired by rotation a new chairman, Aubrey Oxlade. Oxlade was a Sydney lawyer, a conservative, well-meaning man with a deep love of cricket. The retiring chairman, Dr Robertson, was prepared to take a hard line against the MCC and hold out for a guarantee that bodyline would not be bowled in 1934; for Oxlade, however, the first priority was ensuring the 1934 tour went ahead. In a letter to Robertson on 20 June 1933, when Robertson was still chairman, Oxlade said, 'I am fully of the opinion that under no circumstances should the tour of our team in England be abandoned . . . We all realize that tact and careful judgment will have to be exercised by both sides.' When the MCC set its deadline on 12 December Oxlade was stirred to action. He instructed the Board's secretary, Bill Jeanes, to inform the Board's members that he would send a cable confirming the tour would go ahead without further assurances as soon as he had a majority of Board members in favour of it. On 14 December the cable was sent. It read, 'With further reference to your cable on 9 October and your confirmatory cable of 12 December in reply to ours on 16 November, we, too, now regard the position finalised. Our team will leave Australia on 9 March.' On the same day, the MCC replied, 'We are very glad to know we may look forward to welcoming the Australians next summer. We shall do all in our power to make their visit enjoyable.'

Thus, the great bodyline controversy came to an end. Some people in the Australian cricket world believed the Board had caved in under pressure from the MCC, and the former chairman of the Board, Dr Robertson, certainly believed Aubrey Oxlade had overstepped himself. On 15 December, he said in a letter to Jeanes, 'The precipitant action of the chairman renders my reply futile and superfluous, except that it will record my disapproval. Firstly, no team should be sent until a definite promise was received that the methods objected to would be barred.' On the whole, the reaction in both Australia and England was one of relief that it was all over. When the New Year honours were announced a couple of weeks later, Oxlade was among the recipients. He was awarded a CBE, and many people believed at the time that it was a reward for ending the bodyline row. *Punch* magazine made a little joke at Oxlade's expense. It said he would have been elevated to the Order of the Garter if only one could have been found big enough to fit leg-theory.

16
Loose Ends

There were only two loose ends left, Jardine and Larwood. While the final negotiations were going on between the Board of Control and the MCC at the end of 1933, Jardine was leading England in a Test series against the Indians in India. So far as anyone knew, it was Jardine's intention to lead England against the Australians in 1934. That prospect was viewed with dismay on the Australian side. The Board's representative in England, Dr Macdonald, sailed for the United States on 20 October – hardly an opportune time for the Board – but before he left he warned the MCC of the consequences of choosing Jardine as captain in 1934. It is not known whether Macdonald was acting here at the direction of the Board, or whether the warning was an initiative of his own. We do know he had an intense dislike of Jardine. This is what he said to the Board in a letter written after his arrival in America, 'To achieve victory at any cost seems to be an attribute common to both Attila and Mr Jardine. If I do Attila an injustice by this simile I tender an apology to his belated memory.' Macdonald reported to Jeanes that he told the secretary of the MCC, Findlay, that 'there would be an immediate and complete restoration of those amicable relations which, previous to Jardine, had always marked the great Test matches between England and Australia; but that if Jardine was made captain in 1934 the contests would not be England v Australia, or Australia v England, but Jardine v Australia, and Australia v Jardine, and

that under his captaincy there would be a veiled
vendetta.'

There was agitation for Jardine's dismissal from
another quarter. On 5 February 1934, the Governor of
South Australia, Sir Alexander Hore-Ruthven, wrote
a letter on the subject to Pelham Warner, no doubt
expecting that Warner would circulate it among fellow
members of the MCC Committee. The letter, as quoted
by E. W. Swanton in *Follow On*, said in part:

> 'The Jardine question is very important and from what I can
> see from the signs out here, the only thing which could
> disturb the harmony players and public are all anxious to
> maintain would be to put Jardine in charge again. The whole
> atmosphere will be altered if he is made captain. The players
> will go on the field with a feeling of irritation and suspicion
> . . . So if you want the game to be played in the proper spirit
> and the whole controversy buried once and for all, keep
> Jardine out of the picture on any plea you can find. I know
> the difficulties of not appearing to let him down, but the
> question is so vital, not only from the point of view of cricket,
> but of the friendly feeling between the two countries, that
> some excuse must be found for leaving him out. As once a
> sore is opened again it is going to be very difficult to heal,
> and all the soothing syrup we have administered of late will
> be wasted.'

The MCC had a very tricky problem on its hands. Its
choice was to dump Jardine, which would certainly
have caused a public outcry, or to appoint him as
captain on the condition he did not use bodyline tactics.
The MCC would have guessed that Jardine would not
accept such a condition, and the very high probability
was that he would refuse the captaincy, which might
have caused an even bigger outcry. In the end, Jardine
saved the MCC having to make the choice. In March,
while the Australians were already on their way to

England, he announced in India that he had no desire to lead the England side against them. He offered no reason, then or later, for his decision, so we are left to guess why he made it. The simplest explanation is that he learned of the MCC's implicit undertaking to the Australians that bodyline would not be permitted, and he decided that it was impossible for him to captain the side under these circumstances. This would be consistent with the recollection of his daughter, Mrs Lawry, that Jardine felt the MCC had betrayed him. 'My mother used to say he was bitter about it,' Mrs Lawry says. 'There were painful memories.' We do not know, and it would be interesting to know, if the MCC in any way encouraged his decision to stand down.

Towards the end of his stay in India Jardine went on a shooting expedition and bagged two tigers, two panthers, a bear and other animals. He sailed for England late in April, and while he was en route it was rumoured in the London press that he was about to announce his engagement to a Sydney society girl. He was asked about the rumour when he arrived in England, but refused to make a comment. Two weeks later, his engagement was announced – not to a Sydney girl, but to Margaret Peat, the daughter of the senior partner in the international firm of chartered accountants, Peat, Marwick, Mitchell. Jardine was only thirty-three then, but he never played big cricket again. Australians such as Bill O'Reilly who had encountered him in 1932–33 and met him many years later found that he had mellowed with age. O'Reilly had dinner with him after the war and was surprised to find he was actually very shy, as his daughter, Mrs Lawry, says he always had been. In these later years he did not talk much about the bodyline affair, but when he

did it was never with regret. To the end his victory
over the Australians in 1932–33 gave him deep satisfaction. John Arlott remembers him, long after the war,
rubbing his hands and recalling with triumph, 'We did
it, we did it.'

It does not seem he ever softened in his attitude
to Bradman. In October 1957, a Sydney *Sun-Herald*
reporter had a forty-minute interview with Jardine in
his London office. The following is an extract from his
report:

> 'Three times I mentioned the name Bradman . . . Not once
> did he show a flicker of recognition. I asked him to name the
> greatest batsman of his time. "Oh, Jack Hobbs," he said,
> smoking placidly. "No doubt about it. Number one every
> time. He was so good on bad wickets." "Is that why you put
> him above Bradman?" I asked. He looked out of the office
> window across the City's narrow streets and said absently,
> "Hobbs, yes." For him the Bowral boy does not exist.'

Four months after this interview, in February 1958,
Jardine was found to have lung cancer. When he
began to have trouble breathing, he was moved to a
sanatorium in Switzerland. He died there in June that
year, aged fifty-seven.

Harold Larwood continued to play cricket for Nottinghamshire for another five years after the bodyline
tour, but he never played another Test and he never
played again against the Australians. Larwood made
himself available for the first Test against the Australians in 1934 on the grounds that he was not fully fit,
although, as he has since revealed, the real reason was
that he had been placed in an invidious position by
being asked to apologize to the MCC for his bowling
in Australia. Shortly afterwards he declared he would
never play against the Australians again. In *The Larwood Story*, Larwood admits with great frankness that,

quite apart from all this, he had been in two minds about whether to play in the Tests of 1934. 'I didn't want to play against them if it meant I was going to be hit all over the field,' Larwood wrote. '. . . I had humbled them on their own pitches and I didn't want them to humble me in England, especially as they said I was unfair.' Larwood has lived in Australia since 1950, and he has not once expressed regret for his bowling in 1932–33.

Yet a majority of Jardine's men did come to disavow his tactics, or at least to have misgivings about them. Of those who have since died, Pataudi objected to them at the time, and Hammond and Duckworth declared their opposition to them later. It is likely, too, that Tate disliked bodyline, for it was wholly foreign to his style of play. Of those members of Jardine's team who are living, Allen, Wyatt and, apparently, Brown were opposed to bodyline, and Ames has disclosed that he became unhappy about it even before the tour was over. Bowes still thinks bodyline was fair, but he admits it may have been necessary to ban it because of its danger to batsmen. Even Voce, according to one of his team-mates, has come to believe that bodyline was bad for the game. In spite of all this, however, Jardine's players, including one or two who did not like him personally, have remained loyal to him to a man. They revere him still for his courage and his indomitable spirit. Bill Bowes says, simply, 'He was probably the greatest man I ever knew.'

Biographies

Harry Alexander
Nicknamed 'The Bull', Alexander was a strong aggressive and quite fast opening bowler from Victoria, and some saw him as a possible weapon of retaliation against the Englishmen. He did play one Test, the fifth, and hit Jardine a nasty blow on the hip.

Gubby Allen
Born George Oswald Allen in Sydney in July 1902, Allen belonged to a family which had been successful in the legal profession, in business and in politics in Sydney for three generations. Gubby's family moved to England to live while he was still a child, and he was by upbringing (Eton and Cambridge) and manner very English. Allen was technically an all-rounder, but he could bowl much better than he could bat. He was on the short side, but he had a good action and could bowl at a lively place. Larwood believes Allen was actually faster than he was in 1930. He was a close friend and confidant of Pelham Warner, with whom he shared a dislike of Jardine's methods. Allen captained the England team which toured Australia four years later, in 1936–37, a tour which did much to heal the wounds opened by bodyline. After his retirement from the game he became one of the most influential men in the MCC.

Les Ames
Larwood wrote that Duckworth was a better wicket-keeper than Ames, but that Ames was preferred in

1932–33 because of his superior batting. The implication was that skill behind the stumps was not so necessary while the England attack relied on fast bowling. However, Ames retained his position in the England side until 1938 and came to be considered a wicketkeeper of the first rank. Born in 1905, he was of dark complexion and solid build. At the time, he was believed by the Australians to be one of the English players who disagreed with Jardine's tactics. Bill Ponsford says Ames sympathized with him when he was being hit by Larwood and Voce repeatedly in the third Test.

Bill Bowes

Born in 1908, Bowes was still fairly new to big cricket when he was chosen as a late addition to the 1932–33 touring party. Bowes, a Yorkshireman, was 6' 4" (193 cm) tall and rangy of build, but the most distinguishing feature of his appearance was his rimless spectacles. He had an awkward-looking, shambling run to the wicket, and he crossed his right leg behind the left as he went into the delivery stride. There was a lot of wrist in his action and, although he was not fast through the air, he had the ability to make the ball kick off the pitch. But he did not find his feet in Australia in 1932–33 and played in only one Test, the second. His best years were still to come.

Don Bradman

Bradman was born on 27 August 1908, at Cootamundra, but when he was two the family moved to Bowral. It was at Bowral that Bradman spent all of his boyhood and where he first made a name for himself as a batsman of rare ability. His uncle was captain of the Bowral cricket team, and as a boy Bradman followed the team about as a scorer. Once, when the Bowral team was a man short in a match against Moss Vale, Bradman was sent in at the fall of the eighth wicket. He was thirteen years old and still wore short pants, but the Moss Vale men could not get him out, and he was 37 not out at the end of the innings. After devoting himself for a couple of seasons almost entirely to tennis, at which he also showed exceptional promise, he became a regular member of the Bowral cricket team when he was seventeen, and at once began to perform the prodigious scoring feats for which he was soon to become internationally known. Cricket officials in Sydney quickly came to hear of him and when he was eighteen he was brought to the city to play grade cricket. He got into the NSW team when he was nineteen and the Test side when he was twenty. That was in 1928–29, when the Englishmen were in Australia. By the time Jardine's team arrived in Australia in October, 1932, Bradman had stepped up his run-making to the point where he was making a century almost every second time he batted. Bradman was short and of light but athletic build. He had light-brown hair, which some writers described as fair when the sun shone on it and which by 1932 was just beginning to thin. He never smoked, he rarely drank, and he was not gregarious by nature. He had a good ear for music, and he played the piano well enough to be heard in public. After all these years, his fame is undiminished. He is not simply the most famous of all Australian sportsmen; he is quite probably the most famous Australian.

Freddie Brown

Brown captained the England team which toured Australia in 1950–51 and therefore has a fairly prominent place in cricket history. In 1932–33, however, he was a junior and largely inconspicuous member of the side, and he played in none of the Tests. Born in 1910, Brown was a tall, rather heavy man with reddish hair and a bluff, outgoing personality. At Cambridge he won a Blue for hockey as well as cricket, and he was also good at Rugby, squash and golf. Jardine is said to have confiscated his golf sticks during the tour because he believed they were affecting his batting.

Arthur Carr

Born in 1894, Carr had begun playing for Nottinghamshire when he was only sixteen and was the country's captain when Larwood and Voce came together. Carr captained England once in 1926, but blundered dreadfully by sending Australia in and losing the match. Carr had much in common with Jardine: he was an amateur but played the game as hard as any professional, and he had a distaste for Australians.

Claude Corbett

One of Australia's best-known sports writers between the wars. He came from a family of journalists, his father, W. F. Corbett, having been prominent in the profession. Corbett is remembered by a colleague as 'a man of the world' who was 'very wide awake'. In 1932–33 he worked for the Sydney *Sun*.

Ernest Crutchley

A senior British Government officer who was posted to Australia in 1928 and three years later became the head of the British Government mission in Canberra, pending the appointment of Britain's first High Commissioner in Australia. His title was, simply, the British Government's representative in Australia. A diary he kept during the summer of 1932–33 has recently thrown new light on political intervention in the bodyline controversy.

Len Darling

To some extent Darling owed his selection for the last two Tests in 1932–33 to the fact that he was a left-hander. The selectors reasoned, probably correctly, that left-handers would not find bodyline so difficult to handle. Born in 1909, he played his first Test in 1931–32, against South Africa.

George Duckworth

Duckworth had kept wickets for England from 1924 to 1931, but Ames was preferred to him in 1932–33, one reason being he was a better batsman. Some English commentators, including Neville Cardus, were critical of this, believing Duckworth to be still the better keeper. Duckworth was consequently one of the team's 'passengers', playing in only seven first-class matches throughout the summer. Aged thirty-one in 1932–33, he was a short, broad man with a thick crop of fair hair and a ruddy complexion. He was a man of rough and ready humour, inclined to be boisterous, and on the field he was known for his deafening appeals. Legend has it that Duckworth was the first to notice Bradman's alleged discomfort when Larwood made the ball fly at him off a rain-affected pitch in 1930, which some say provided Jardine with the inspiration for his bodyline strategy.

Percy Fender

Fender played for England briefly and not too success-fully immediately after the First World War, but he is better remembered as an outstanding leader of the

Surrey team in the 1920s and early 1930s. Born in August 1892, he was something of a dasher with the bat and bowled leg-breaks and googlies.

Jack Fingleton

Bodyline was possibly a bigger setback to Fingleton than to any other Australian. He was a young (twenty-four years old) batsman on the rise, and after his early successes against Jardine's men he must have had expectations of further success in the Tests to come. Fingleton was a mainly defensive batsman, not at all exciting to watch, and he was not naturally suited to handling bodyline, for he was neither quick on his feet nor strong on the hook shot. He fought his way back into the Australian team three years later and was a regular member of the side in the mid- and late 1930s. Fingleton had worked as a journalist since his teens, and in the mid-1940s he wrote a book about the bodyline controversy called *Cricket Crisis*. Many critics consider it the finest cricket book ever written by an Australian.

Eddie Gilbert

An Aboriginal fast bowler of express speed who played for Queensland in the early 1930s. Born at the Cherbourg Aboriginal mission north of Brisbane in 1908, Gilbert became part of the Queensland team in 1930–31, and in the following season achieved national fame by knocking the bat from Don Bradman's hands and then getting him out for a duck. Bradman said Gilbert was the fastest bowler he ever saw, but it was widely believed that he obtained his extra speed with an illegal action. He was no-balled for throwing eleven times in three overs in Melbourne in December 1931, and his reputation was tainted thereafter. He made a brief return to Brisbane club cricket immediately after the Second World War, but not many years later he was admitted to the Goodna mental hospital near Brisbane, where he spent the rest of his life. He died in 1978.

Clarrie Grimmett

One of the most successful of all Australian spin bowlers, Grimmett was strangely unsuccessful in the Tests of 1932–33, taking only five wickets in the first three Tests and being dropped for the last two. He was forty-one then and it must have seemed to many that his Test career was at an end, but he returned to play in two more series for Australia, in 1934 and in 1935–36.

Hunter Hendry

Born in 1895, Hendry played as an all-rounder for Australia from 1921 to 1928–29. He was, and is, generally known by his nickname, Stork – a name given to him by M. A. Noble not because of his height (6′ 2″, or 188 cm) but because of his habit of standing on one leg in slips. Hendry came from Sydney but later moved to Melbourne and played for Victoria.

Wally Hammond

Hammond was undoubtedly the premier batsman of the England team in 1932–33, but the public's attention was so concentrated on the English fast bowlers that Hammond, for once, seemed to recede into the background. When the Englishmen toured Australia four years earlier, Hammond, then aged twenty-five, caused a sensation by scoring 905 runs in the Test series at an average of 113.2. This was a record aggregate for a series, and it seemed a record that would stand for many years – until Don Bradman broke it eighteen months later. Bradman had the better of Hammond even in 1932–33. Although Hammond scored two centuries in the Tests and was reckoned to have had a successful series and although Bradman was reckoned to have failed, Bradman still averaged more than Hammond, 56.57 to 55.00. Hammond seemed to be a supporter of Jardine's tactics in Australia – the umpire George Hele wrote of one occasion on which Hammond apparently led the other English players into the bodyline cordon – but he became a strong opponent of bodyline after it was bowled at him in 1933.

Bruce Harris

Harris was a tennis writer for the *Evening Standard* and had little knowledge of cricket, but he was sent to cover the Tests of 1932–33 apparently because of his wide experience, being preferred to a young cricket writer on the paper named E. W. Swanton, later to become one of the most outstanding of the game's chroniclers. Harris managed to win Jardine's confidence and throughout the tour served as a kind of mouthpiece for him, and many Australians later blamed his one-sided reporting for the ignorance about bodyline which prevailed in England. After returning to England Harris wrote a book about the tour called *Jardine Justified*, which, as the title suggests, presented only the English side of the dispute.

Jack Hobbs

Hobbs's marvellous cricket career was only just ending when he came to Australia in 1932–33 as a cricket writer for the London *Star*. He had played his last Test as recently as 1930 and was still playing county cricket, and when it was reported that he was bringing his cricket gear with him on the tour some Australians believed he might be recalled to the English team if the need arose. The need did not arise, and Hobbs spent the tour in the press box, writing articles which were rarely critical of Jardine's tactics, even if they did not wholeheartedly support him. In fact, the actual writing was done by another journalist, Jack Ingham, whom the *Star* sent along as Hobbs's 'ghost'. Hobbs declared his opposition to bodyline forcefully enough after the tour, and his failure to do so at the time is not easy to understand, even allowing for the fact that he was by nature averse to all kinds of controversy. Perhaps he still felt so close to the English team that he might have considered criticism of their bowling to amount to disloyalty. Born in December 1882, Hobbs had made his Test debut in 1907–08 and was considered England's master batsman for the next twenty years. He did not retire from first-class cricket until 1935, when he was fifty-two.

Bert Ironmonger

At forty-nine, he was by a long way the oldest player in the Tests of 1932–33. Ironmonger was a left-arm, leg-break bowler who spun the ball so much that batsmen were said to be able to hear the ball humming towards them. The extraordinary feature of his career was that, having played for Queensland as early as 1909, he did not get into the Test side until 1928–29, when he was forty-five. Ironmonger was a big, heavy man who was given the nickname Dainty because of his bulk and clumsiness. He had the tops of the first two fingers of his bowling hand missing, but the callouses which grew on the stumps were said to be a big help to him in spinning the ball. Ironmonger grew up on a dairy farm near Ipswich, and he bore the stamp of the country, with its rough and ready manners, for the rest of his life. He moved to Victoria, and most of his big cricket was played there.

Archie Jackson

Born in Scotland in September 1909, Jackson came to Australia with his family when he was two. He was a brilliant boy cricketer and won a place in the NSW side in 1926–27, when he was only seventeen. Thus, a year younger than Bradman, he got into big cricket a year ahead of him. Jackson came to the fore only eleven years after death took Victor Trumper out of the game, and at that time the Australian cricket public still hoped for the appearance of another Trumper, just as since 1948 it has hoped for the appearance of another Bradman. The fact that Jackson, a stylish and naturally graceful batsman, reminded so many people of Trumper probably helps to explain why Australian cricket followers were so enthusiastic about him. In fact, his first Test in 1928–29, in which he scored 164, proved to be the high point of his career. After losing form, Jackson was found to have tuberculosis at the end of 1931, and he died from the disease in Brisbane on 15 February 1933, while the fourth Test of the bodyline series was being played there.

Douglas Jardine

Jardine was born in October 1900, in India, where his father, Malcolm, was a prominent lawyer. The Jardines were of Scottish stock, and Jardine always considered himself a Scotsman, not an Englishman. Jardine had a lonely upbringing. He was an only child, and when he was still a small boy his parents sent him to a preparatory school in England named Horris Hill and later to one of the most exclusive schools in the country,

Winchester. Jardine excelled at cricket at school and afterwards at Oxford, but he did not play regularly after leaving university, apparently because he was devoting himself to his career. He did not play in a Test until he came to Australia in Percy Chapman's team in 1928–29. He was a tall, sinewy man with Basil Rathbone features; his height was generally given as 6′ 2″ (188 cm). He spoke with a clipped, upper-class accent and he smoked a pipe, although not habitually. His favourite relaxation was trout-fishing, and he also enjoyed game-shooting. The characteristics of his personality have been drawn by so many writers over the years that he has, in a literary sense, become a kind of caricature. He was, by all accounts, withdrawn, taciturn, introverted, tense, superior, self-willed and completely inflexible. Yet those who knew him well also found him shy, considerate and witty. Undeniably, he was a born leader. He led his players into one of the most violent storms in the history of sport, in some cases against their will, yet he did not lose the loyalty of one of them.

M. R. Jardine

According to Douglas Jardine's daughter, Mrs Fianach Lawry, Jardine had a specially strong attachment to and admiration for his father, Malcolm, and it may well be that Douglas was motivated to some extent by a desire to emulate him, for up to a point he followed closely in his father's footsteps. Malcolm Jardine, widely known in the cricket world as M. R. Jardine, was born in India in 1869, shone as a schoolboy cricketer in England and went on to Oxford, where he studied law and won a Blue for cricket in his first year. Douglas did all this, too, although he did not enjoy the distinction, as his father did, of captaining Oxford.

M. R. Jardine worked as a lawyer in India from 1894 until 1916, and for a time was Advocate-General in Bombay. He was living at Walton-on-Thames at least as early as the mid-1920s, and he was certainly living there in 1932 when Percy Fender visited Douglas there to discuss cricket tactics. When M. R. Jardine died in 1947 he was vice-president of the Surrey club. His wife, Alison, died in 1936.

Alan Kippax

Born in 1897, Kippax moved into the first rank of Australian batsmen in the late 1920s, and in the 1930 Tests against England he was the most successful of them after Bradman. Tall (6' or 183 cm) and slim, he was a graceful strokemaker after the manner of Victor Trumper, whom he seemed to imitate even to the point of having his sleeves rolled up just beyond the wrist. In his prime, he had been a fine hooker of fast bowling, but he had twice been hit in the head in the summer before Jardine's team arrived and his confidence was shaken. In 1933, he wrote, or at least helped to write, a book called *Anti-Bodyline*, which was a reasoned condemnation of Jardine's tactics and was frequently quoted in the debate about bodyline which followed.

Harold Larwood

Larwood was born (on 14 November 1904), raised in, and began his working life as a miner in the Nottinghamshire mining village, Nuncargate. It was his great talent for fast bowling which enabled him to escape the pits. On the strength of his fine performances in local cricket, he was signed on as a professional by the Notts county club when he was nineteen, one of his first duties being to clean the boots of the senior players. He got into the county side at the age of twenty and into the Test side in 1926, when he was twenty-one. He toured Australia in 1928–29 with moderate success, and in 1930 he was given such a mauling by Bradman that he was dropped for one Test. His success with bodyline, especially against Bradman, was therefore a sweet revenge. Larwood was only 5′ 7½″ (171 cm) tall, but was strongly and broadly built. His nickname was Lol, although Jardine, at least, always called him Harold. Some of the Australians used to call him the Little Miner. He was quiet, almost diffident in manner, but on the field with the ball in his hand he was extremely aggressive. Some of the Australians believed there was a real element of spite in Larwood's bowling in 1932–33. He was avenging himself for past indignities, and he seemed to take pleasure in doing it. His bowling action was magnificent. Old newsreel films of it are thrilling to watch. George Hele, one of the umpires in 1932–33, said Larwood glided to the wicket so quietly that he could not hear him coming.

P. K. Lee

Born in 1904, Lee was an all-rounder from South Australia. He bowled off-breaks at a quickish pace, and batted capably in the middle order. He had played one Test against South Africa in 1930–31, and was brought into the side for the last of the bodyline Tests. He actually bowled the last ball of the series, which was hit by Hammond for six.

Maurice Leyland

Born in 1900, Leyland seemed to typify Yorkshire cricket. He was dour, down-to-earth and full of determination and fighting spirit, yet possessed a wry sense of humour. He was a solid left-handed batsman, more effective than elegant, of whom Ian Peebles once wrote, 'All his movements were weighty and decided.' He was of medium height and broad in the beam and deep of chest, and, according to Neville Cardus, his forearms resembled Yorkshire hams. The 1932–33 series was his third against Australia.

Joseph Lyons

Prime Minister of Australia at the time of the flare-up over bodyline. Born in Tasmania in 1879, Lyons was a Labor Premier of Tasmania in the 1920s but after moving into Federal Parliament he resigned from the Labor Party and led the United Australian Party to victory in December 1931. He was fond of sport in general, and of cricket in particular, and he used to stay up late at night to listen to broadcasts from Tests in England. He was of Irish extraction, but he was also an Anglophile and a loyalist.

Stan McCabe

It needs to be appreciated that in 1932–33 McCabe had not acquired the great reputation he enjoyed later in his career. Although he had played against England in 1930, he was still a comparative newcomer, only twenty-two years old, who had yet to really establish himself. Until he played his wonderful innings of 187 not out in the first Test, he had not made a Test 50. McCabe came from Grenfell, NSW, and he had the easy-going manner of someone raised in the country. He was 5′ 8″ (173 cm) tall and weighed 10 stone 6 pounds (66.2 kg) in 1932–33. His hair was balding and his eyes, according to one account, were 'sad blue'. Like Bradman, he was a good golfer (his handicap was eight) and a good billiards player. Jack Fingleton wrote that he did not think McCabe really enjoyed playing

Test cricket, for he did not easily bear the nervous strain of it, yet there was generally a light-hearted quality about his batting. It is said he never slowed down his scoring when he got into the 90s.

Tom Mitchell

A googly bowler from Derbyshire, who got through his overs at remarkable speed, sometimes taking as little as 100 seconds to bowl six balls. He was a coalminer by occupation, and had spent part of the previous winter, 1931–32, working underground. A small, bespectacled man, who was especially short in the legs, Mitchell was considered the humorist of the touring side. On the field he was excitable, given to shrill appeals and to displays of anguish when he beat the batsman but did not take a wicket. Mitchell played in the fourth Test in place of the injured Voce, and he took three wickets and caught Bradman at point when Bradman seemed on the verge of a big innings.

Lisle Nagel

At the start of the 1932–33 season, Nagel was not even a contender for a place in the Australian side, but he suddenly found himself playing in the first Test on the strength of his sensational performance for the Australian XI against the MCC, in which he took 8 for 32. It was the only Test he played in his career. Nagel, a Victorian, was a medium-pace, right-arm bowler. He was extremely tall (6′ 6″ or 198 cm), but he brought his arm over too low to gain much advantage from his height. Nagel had a brother, Vernon, an inch shorter than himself, who also played for Victoria.

Leo O'Brien

O'Brien never quite fulfilled the great promise he showed when he first appeared on the cricket scene in the early 1930s, and he failed in three of the four innings he played against Jardine's men. However, one of the umpires in the series, George Hele, numbered O'Brien among the Australian batsmen who stood in the line of the bouncers.

Bert Oldfield

Oldfield had come to the fore in cricket in the AIF team during the First World War, so he was already a veteran, thirty-five years old, in 1932–33. He was a short (5′ 7″, or 167 cm), neat, trim figure, and his wicketkeeping was smart, snappy, precise, although not ostentatious. He used to have some trouble with his fingers, and to protect them he wore two pairs of water-soaked chamois inner gloves as well as special casings around his fingers. Oldfield played his first Test in 1920–21 and his last in 1936–37. Among Australian wicketkeepers, he is ranked as one of the all-time greats.

Bill O'Reilly

O'Reilly was the only Australian who could have looked back on the 1932–33 series with real satisfaction. He took 27 wickets in the Tests, far more than any other Australian bowler, and he played a key part in Australia's only victory in the second Test. Although he turned twenty-eight during the series, O'Reilly was relatively new to Test cricket, having made his debut for Australia only in the summer before, against the South Africans. It was in 1932–33 that his reputation as a leg-spin bowler of exceptional class was established. O'Reilly was a tall (6′ 3″, or 191 cm) and gangly figure, and his bowling action was described as vigorous confusion of arms and legs. On the field he was intensely competitive, always ready to show his anger, with the heavens and with himself, when things did not go his way. O'Reilly was widely regarded as the world's best bowler in the 1930s, and today he is still one of the game's outstanding personalities.

Nawab of Pataudi

Pataudi was an Indian prince who had come to England to further his education in 1926, when he was sixteen, and yet seemed to devote most of his energy to improving his cricket. He was coached by the famous Kent batsman Frank Woolley before moving to Oxford. He won his Blue for cricket there in 1929, and in 1931 made 238 not out against Cambridge, a record for the university match. He was only twenty-two when he came to Australia, and he was deeply offended by insults shouted by barrackers.

Eddie Paynter

Paynter did not play many Tests against Australia, but he was outstandingly successful in the ones he did play, averaging 84.42 over his career. Born in 1901, he was a short man and quick on his feet, and he batted with the grit one would expect of a Lancashire professional. He did not play in the first two Tests in 1932–33, and he was brought into the third mainly because of Bill O'Reilly's success in the second: it was thought that, as a left-hander, Paynter would be better able to handle O'Reilly's spin. He did everything that was expected of him and, in fact, averaged more in the Tests than any other player, on either side.

Bill Ponsford

Ponsford scored so heavily in the 1920s that, until Bradman came along, he was considered Australia's number-one batsman. He is still the only batsman ever to have made two first-class scores of more than 400. Born in October 1900, he got into the Victorian side in 1920–21 and into the Australian side in 1924–25. Ponsford was a heavily built man, and he used a bat weighing 2 pounds 12 ounces, which was exceptionally heavy in his day. Although he was a specialist opener, he looked at his best when playing spin, and his footwork then was sharp and precise. He was a man of a modest, retiring nature, not given to saying more than was necessary.

Vic Richardson

At thirty-eight years of age, Richardson was the oldest of the Australian batsmen who faced the bodyline attack, yet until he made two ducks in the last Test he seemed to handle it better than most. Richardson was an enterprising batsman with a fondness for the hook shot, but he seems to have had flaws of technique which were blamed for his lack of success in Tests generally. Richardson was one of the personalities of the Australian team – extroverted, full of zest, red-blooded. He was the Australian most in favour of using bodyline in retaliation, yet he is said to have been one of the few Australians who continued to mix socially with the English players. Richardson captained South Australia from 1921 to 1935, and he captained Australia once, on the tour of South Africa in 1935–36. He is the grandfather of the Chappell brothers. He died in 1969.

Dr Allen Robertson

Robertson, of Victoria, became chairman of the Board of Control in September 1930, and held the position until September 1933. He was therefore the most

senior cricket administrator in Australia when the row
over bodyline came to a head.

Herbert Sutcliffe

Sutcliffe's batting was not unlike the man himself –
dogged, unostentatious, deadly serious and yet possessing a certain natural dignity. He played the game
hard, and the Australians believed he was the most
enthusiastic supporter in the English team of Jardine's
tactics. At times he seemed to initiate the placement
of the bodyline field. Bill O'Reilly says, 'He was
undoubtedly Douglas Jardine's right-hand man. As
head of the professionals on tour, his advice was sought
much more often than that of Bob Wyatt, his vice-
captain.' Sutcliffe, a Yorkshireman, was born in
November 1894, which means he turned thirty-eight as
the tour began. In the 1920s he and Jack Hobbs opened
the batting for England with great success. He was of
medium height and solid build, and his black hair was
always neatly parted and combed. Because of his rather
lordly manner, he was sometimes called the 'aristocrat'
of professional cricket. O'Reilly wrote that even if he
beat him completely with a good ball Sutcliffe 'would
throw back his head, look straight down his nose and
leave you with the impression that it was barely worth
the effort to shape up to you.'

Maurice Tate

Tate was thirty-seven years old when he came to
Australia in 1932–33 and his best years were certainly
behind him, but he might still have been a force in the
English side if Jardine had not fixed upon fast leg-
theory as his master-plan for beating the Australians.
Tate was a medium-pace bowler and, as such, was
virtually a supernumerary in 1932–33. In the 1920s he

was England's premier bowler, and he would still be counted among the best medium-pacers the game has known. Tate was a tall, lumbering man with big feet and a genial disposition. He was prone to jumbling his syllables, for instance saying 'stanima' instead of 'stamina'. Pelham Warner wrote that Tate remained cheerful throughout the tour, in spite of the fact he played in only five games, fewer than any other Englishman, yet it is hard to believe his pride was not hurt by being unwanted.

Jimmy Thomas

Thomas, a Welshman of working-class background, was a tough-talking, high-living Labour politician, who at the time of the bodyline dispute was Secretary for the Dominions, a Cabinet position which gave him special responsibility for Britain's relations with Australia.

Hedley Verity

Verity was such an outstanding figure in international cricket for most of the 1930s that it is easy to forget he was virtually an unknown when he came to Australia in 1932–33. Although he was twenty-seven years old, he had secured his place in the Yorkshire side only two years earlier. He was a tall (6', or 183 cm), fair-haired, left-arm spinner. He was not a slow bowler, however; his pace was only slightly below medium, and occasionally he could whip down a ball of genuine pace. He had a longish, elegant run to the wicket and a graceful action. Johnnie Moyes wrote of him, 'Verity the man seemed aloof, but he was not – it was merely that he was not given to hilarity. Neither garrulous nor taciturn, he had a fund of humour that showed itself on suitable occasions. There were, in fact, profound depths of character in this man.' Verity was wounded on active service in the Second World War – and died of his wounds in an Italian prisoner-of-war camp in 1943, aged thirty-eight.

Bill Voce

Like Larwood, Voce began his life as a Nottinghamshire miner. He was a big man, tall and broad and possessing great strength. He was a left-arm bowler with a fine loose action, but he was not particularly fast. Bill O'Reilly says his speed was about the same as Terry Alderman's, although Gubby Allen insists he was quicker than that. He was only twenty-three when he came to Australia in 1932–33, and he bowled bodyline for Jardine with a youthful fervour. Larwood was his constant companion. Arthur Carr, the Notts captain, wrote of the two of them, 'They are bosom friends. Harold looks after Bill like a father and Bill looks after him.'

Tim Wall

Wall was Australia's leading fast bowler in 1932–33, but his lack of real pace made him an ineffective counter to Larwood. Born in May 1904, Wall was a tall, thin, bespectacled man, reserved by nature and gentlemanly of manner. He was, like O'Reilly and Woodfull, a schoolteacher. He had a long run to the wicket, which seemed to be even longer because he tended to walk back to his mark slowly. Bradman rated him very highly as a bowler while the ball was new.

Pelham Warner

Warner was born in October 1873, which means he was fifty-nine during the 1932–33 tour, an age at which he would have much preferred plain sailing to weathering tempests. Like Jardine, Warner was born abroad into a family of colonial lawyers, in his case in Trinidad, and like Jardine he studied law at Oxford and made a big impression there as a cricketer. In 1892, when he was only eighteen, he became a member of the MCC, thereby beginning a lifelong association with that body. In 1903, although he had never up to that time played a Test, he was chosen to captain the England team touring Australia in the following summer. He also captained the England team which toured Australia in 1911–12, although he was laid up by illness for most of the tour. Despite his age, he continued playing for his county, Middlesex, after the war, finally retiring at 6.22 P.M. on 31 August 1920, when Middlesex beat Surrey at Lord's to win the county championship. Thereafter, he was active as a cricket official, serving as both an England selector and an MCC Committee member. He was, in fact, one of the leading lights of the MCC between the wars, and eventually he became its president. He was of medium height or a little under; he must have given an impression of smallness, for he was sometimes referred to as 'little Plummy'. He had a fresh, pink complexion, which made him look younger than his years, but he had been bald since his Oxford days. His nickname was Plum, and throughout his life he was scarcely known by any other name. The name had no personal significance – it was just a standard degeneration of Pelham. From 1921 to 1934 he wrote on cricket for the *Morning Post*, and he was also the editor of a leading cricket magazine. One of his hobbies was studying naval and military strategy. Warner was genteel, urbane, gentlemanly. His love and reverence for cricket was unbounded. He was knighted in 1937, and he died in 1963, aged 89.

Rockley Wilson

Born in 1879, Wilson was a great character in cricket, even if he was never a great cricketer, and his anecdotes and sayings were widely quoted. Wilson played one Test against Australia in 1920–21, and he made a name for himself afterwards as a coach. Jardine, at Winchester, was one of his pupils.

Bill Woodfull

As captain of the team which had to contend with bodyline, Woodfull was a man under pressure throughout the summer of 1932–33. There was always a possibility he might be considered not strong enough to counter Jardine, but it does not seem that suggestion was ever made. A man of dignity and character, Woodfull seems to have been much respected by all his players. Born in August 1897, he was a rather ponderous but highly effective opening batsman; his range of shots was limited, but his defence was extremely strong. He had played for Australia since 1926 and had been captain since 1930. Woodfull was a man of medium height and fleshy build. He was the son of a Methodist minister and did not drink or smoke, and was conservative in his attitude generally. School-teaching was his profession, and one of his team-mates remembers him as a 'typical schoolmaster'.

Bob Wyatt

Wyatt was captain of England before Jardine, in 1930, and he was captain after him, in 1934. It is reasonable to speculate that if Bradman had not been so awesomely successful in 1930 and if the MCC had not decided that a man of Jardine's mettle was needed to contend with Australia's new strength Wyatt would have been captain in 1932–33, too. If so, there would have been no bodyline. Wyatt was much different in type from his captain. He was a popular, if not colourful, personality, whom Bruce Harris described on that tour as being 'invariably sanguine, good-humoured and friendly'. Born in 1901, Wyatt was the only amateur in the side who had not been to Oxford or Cambridge. He had a fondness for Maori and Hawaiian music, ice-skating, photography and animals. He was a mainly defensive batsman, and generally he fielded in the deep.

Appendix A

Scoring Rates in the Tests

Rates expressed as runs scored for each six balls faced.
Australian players are denoted by **bold** type.

Alexander	5.67	Allen	2.29
Lee	5.26	Paynter	2.26
Bradman	4.49	Sutcliffe	2.22
Larwood	4.02	Bowes	2.18
Darling	3.65	**Nagel**	2.10
O'Reilly	3.59	Wyatt	2.04
McCabe	3.58	**Wall**	2.03
O'Brien	3.11	**Fingleton**	1.98
Richardson	2.80	Ames	1.85
Ironmonger	2.69	Voce	1.85
Grimmett	2.65	**Woodfull**	1.84
Kippax	2.61	Jardine	1.52
Hammond	2.47	Pataudi	1.48
Bromley	2.41	Verity	1.47
Oldfield	2.39	**Love**	1.26
Ponsford	2.38	Mitchell	—
Leyland	2.34		

Author's note. The above list shows in a most striking way that the Australians scored much faster on the whole than the Englishmen. Bradman was easily the fastest of the specialist batsmen, and Jardine and Pataudi the slowest.

Appendix B

1932–33 TEST SERIES

FIRST TEST

AUSTRALIA

W. M. Woodfull	c Ames b Voce	7	b Larwood	0
W. H. Ponsford	b Larwood	32	b Voce	2
J. H. Fingleton	c Allen b Larwood	26	c Voce b Larwood	40
A. F. Kippax	lbw b Larwood	8	b Larwood	19
S. J. McCabe	not out	187	lbw b Hammond	32
V. Y. Richardson	c Hammond b Voce	49	c Voce b Hammond	0
W. A. Oldfield	c Ames b Larwood	4	c Leyland b Larwood	1
C. V. Grimmett	c Ames b Voce	19	c Allen b Larwood	5
L. E. Nagel	b Larwood	0	not out	1
W. J. O'Reilly	b Voce	4	b Voce	7
T. W. Wall	c Allen b Hammond	4	c Ames b Allen	20
	Sundries	20	Sundries	17
Total		360		164

	O	M	R	W	O	M	R	W
Larwood	31	5	96	5	18	4	28	5
Voce	29	4	110	4	17.3	5	54	2
Allen	15	1	65	0	9	5	13	1
Hammond	14.2	0	34	1	15	6	37	2
Verity	13	4	35	0	4	1	15	0

ENGLAND

H. Sutcliffe	lbw b Wall	194	not out	1
R. E. S. Wyatt	lbw b Grimmett	38	not out	0
W. R. Hammond	c Grimmett b Nagel	112		
Nawab of Pataudi	b Nagel	102		
M. Leyland	c Oldfield b Wall	0		
D. R. Jardine	c Oldfield b McCabe	27		
H. Verity	lbw b Wall	2		
G. O. Allen	c & b O'Reilly	19		
L. E. G. Ames	c McCabe b O'Reilly	0		
H. Larwood	lbw b O'Reilly	0		
W. Voce	not out	0		
	Sundries	30		
Total		524	(0 wkts)	1

	O	M	R	W	O	M	R	W
Wall	38	4	104	3				
Nagel	43.4	9	110	2				
O'Reilly	67	32	117	3				
Grimmett	64	22	118	1				
McCabe	15	2	42	1	0.1	0	1	0

England won by ten wickets

SECOND TEST
AUSTRALIA

J. H Fingleton	b Allen	83	c Ames b Allen	1
W. M. Woodfull	b Allen	10	c Allen b Larwood	26
L. P. O'Brien	run out	10	b Larwood	11
D. G. Bradman	b Bowes	0	not out	103
S. J. McCabe	c Jardine b Voce	32	b Allen	0
V. Y. Richardson	c Hammond b Voce	34	lbw b Hammond	32
W. A. Oldfield	not out	27	b Voce	6
C. V. Grimmett	c Sutcliffe b Voce	2	c b Voce	0
T. W. Wall	run out	1	lbw b Hammond	3
W. J. O'Reilly	b Larwood	15	c Ames b Hammond	0
H. Ironmonger	b Larwood	4	run out	0
	Sundries	10	Sundries	9
Total		228		191

	O	M	R	W	O	M	R	W
Larwood	20.3	2	52	2	15	2	50	2
Voce	20	3	54	3	15	2	47	2
Allen	17	3	41	2	12	1	44	2
Hammond	10	3	21	0	10.5	2	21	3
Bowes	19	2	50	1	4	0	20	0

ENGLAND

H. Sutcliffe	c Richardson b Wall	52	b O'Reilly	33
R. E. S. Wyatt	lbw b O'Reilly	13	lbw b O'Reilly	25
W. R. Hammond	b Wall	8	c O'Brien b O'Reilly	23
Nawab of Pataudi	b O'Reilly	15	c Fingleton b Ironmonger	5
M. Leyland	b O'Reilly	22	b Wall	19
D. R. Jardine	c Oldfield b Wall	1	c McCabe b Ironmonger	0
L. E. G. Ames	b Wall	4	c Fingleton b O'Reilly	2
G. O. Allen	c Richardson b O'Reilly	30	st Oldfield b Ironmonger	23
H. Larwood	b O'Reilly	9	c Wall b Ironmonger	4
W. Voce	c McCabe b Grimmett	6	c O'Brien b O'Reilly	0
W. E. Bowes	not out	4	not out	0
	Sundries	5	Sundries	5
Total		169		139

	O	M	R	W	O	M	R	W
Wall	21	4	52	4	8	2	23	1
O'Reilly	34.3	17	63	5	24	5	66	5
Grimmett	16	4	21	1	4	0	19	0
Ironmonger	14	4	28	0	19.1	8	26	4

Australia won by 111 runs

THIRD TEST

ENGLAND

H. Sutcliffe	c Wall b O'Reilly	9	c sub. b Wall		7
D. R. Jardine	b Wall	3	lbw b Ironmonger		56
W. R. Hammond	c Oldfield b Wall	2	b Bradman		85
L. E. G. Ames	b Ironmonger	3	b O'Reilly		69
M. Leyland	b O'Reilly	83	c Wall b Ironmonger		42
R. E. S. Wyatt	c Richardson b Grimmett	78	c Wall b O'Reilly		49
E. Paynter	c Fingleton b Wall	77	not out		1
G. O. Allen	lbw b Grimmett	15	lbw b Grimmett		15
H. Verity	c Richardson b Wall	45	lbw b O'Reilly		40
W. Voce	b Wall	8	b O'Reilly		8
H. Larwood	not out	3	c Bradman b Ironmonger		8
	Sundries	15	Sundries		32
Total		341			412

	O	M	R	W	O	M	R	W
Wall	34.1	10	72	5	29	6	75	1
O'Reilly	50	19	82	2	50.3	21	79	4
Ironmonger	20	6	50	1	57	21	87	3
Grimmett	28	6	94	2	35	9	74	1
McCabe	14	3	28	0	16	0	42	0
Bradman					4	0	23	1

AUSTRALIA

J. H. Fingleton	c Ames b Allen	0	b Larwood		0
W. M. Woodfull	b Allen	22	not out		73
D. G. Bradman	c Allen b Larwood	8	c & b Verity		66
S. J. McCabe	c Jardine b Larwood	8	c Leyland b Allen		7
W. H. Ponsford	b Voce	85	c Jardine b Larwood		3
V. Y. Richardson	b Allen	28	c Allen b Larwood		21
W. A. Oldfield	retired hurt	41	absent hurt		0
C. V. Grimmett	c Voce b Allen	10	b Allen		6
T. W. Wall	b Hammond	6	b Allen		0
W. J. O'Reilly	b Larwood	0	b Larwood		5
H. Ironmonger	not out	0	b Allen		0
	Sundries	14	Sundries		12
Total		222			193

	O	M	R	W	O	M	R	W
Larwood	25	6	55	3	19	3	71	4
Allen	23	4	71	4	17.2	5	50	4
Hammond	17.4	4	30	1	9	3	27	0
Voce	14	5	21	1	4	1	7	0
Verity	16	7	31	0	20	12	26	1

England won by 338 runs

FOURTH TEST

AUSTRALIA

V. Y. Richardson	st Ames b Hammond	83	c Jardine b Verity	32
W. M. Woodfull	b Mitchell	67	c Hammond b Mitchell ...	19
D. G. Bradman	b Larwood	76	c Mitchell b Larwood	24
S. J. McCabe	c Jardine b Allen	20	b Verity	22
W. H. Ponsford	b Larwood	19	c Larwood b Allen	0
L. S. Darling	c Ames b Allen	17	run out	39
E. H. Bromley	c Verity b Larwood	26	c Hammond b Allen	7
H. S. Love	lbw b Mitchell	5	lbw b Larwood	3
T. W. Wall	not out	6	c Jardine b Allen	2
W. J. O'Reilly	b Hammond b Larwood ..	6	b Larwood	4
H. Ironmonger	st Ames b Hammond	8	not out	0
	Sundries	7	Sundries	23
Total		340		175

	O	M	R	W	O	M	R	W
Larwood	31	7	101	4	17.3	3	49	3
Allen	24	4	83	2	17	3	44	3
Hammond	23	5	61	2	10	4	18	0
Mitchell	16	5	49	2	5	0	11	1
Verity	27	12	39	0	19	6	30	2

ENGLAND

D. R. Jardine	c Love b O'Reilly	46	lbw b Ironmonger	24
H. Sutcliffe	lbw b O'Reilly	86	c Darling b Wall	2
W. R. Hammond	b McCabe	20	c Bromley b Ironmonger .	14
R. E. S. Wyatt	c Love b Ironmonger	12		
M. Leyland	c Bradman b O'Reilly	12	c McCabe b O'Reilly	86
L. E. G. Ames	c Darling b Ironmonger ..	17	not out	14
G. O. Allen	c Love b Wall	13		
E. Paynter	c Richardson b Ironmonger	83	not out	14
H. Larwood	b McCabe	23		
H. Verity	not out	23		
T. B. Mitchell	lbw b O'Reilly	0		
	Sundries	21	Sundries	8
Total		356	(4 wkts)	162

	O	M	R	W	O	M	R	W
Wall	33	6	66	1	7	1	17	1
O'Reilly	67.4	27	120	4	30	11	65	1
Ironmonger	43	19	69	3	35	13	47	2
McCabe	23	7	40	2	7.4	2	25	0
Bromley	10	4	19	0				
Bradman	7	1	17	0				
Darling	2	0	4	0				

England won by 6 wickets

FIFTH TEST

AUSTRALIA

V. Y. Richardson	c Jardine b Larwood	0	c Allen b Larwood	0
W. M. Woodfull	b Larwood	14	b Allen	67
D. G. Bradman	b Larwood	48	b Verity	71
L. P. O'Brien	c Larwood b Voce	61	c Verity b Voce	5
S. J. McCabe	c Hammond b Verity	73	c Jardine b Voce	4
L. S. Darling	b Verity	85	c Wyatt b Verity	7
W. A. Oldfield	run out	52	c Wyatt b Verity	5
P. K. Lee	c Jardine b Verity	42	b Allen	15
W. J. O'Reilly	b Allen	19	b Verity	1
H. H. Alexander	not out	17	lbw b Verity	0
H. Ironmonger	b Larwood	1	not out	0
Total	Sundries	23	Sundries	7
		435		182

	O	M	R	W	O	M	R	W
Larwood	32	10	98	4	11	0	44	1
Voce	24	4	80	1	10	0	34	2
Allen	25	1	128	1	11.4	2	54	2
Verity	17	3	62	3	19	9	33	5
Wyatt	2	0	12	0				

ENGLAND

D. R. Jardine	c Oldfield b O'Reilly	18	c Richardson b Ironmonger	24
H. Sutcliffe	c Richardson b O'Reilly ..	56		
W. R. Hammond	lbw b Lee	101	not out	75
H. Larwood	c Ironmonger b Lee	98		
M. Leyland	run out	42	b Ironmonger	0
R. E. S. Wyatt	c Ironmonger b O'Reilly .	51	not out	61
L. E. G. Ames	run out	4		
E. Paynter	b Lee	9		
G. O. Allen	c Bradman b Lee	48		
H. Verity	c Oldfield b Alexander ...	4		
W. Voce	not out	7		
	Sundries	16	Sundries	8
		454	(2 wkts)	168

	O	M	R	W	O	M	R	W
Alexander	35	1	129	1	11	2	25	0
McCabe	12	1	27	0	5	2	10	0
O'Reilly	45	7	100	3	15	5	32	0
Ironmonger	31	13	64	0	26	12	34	2
Lee	40.2	11	111	4	12.2	3	52	0
Darling	7	5	3	0	2	0	7	0
Bradman	1	0	4	0				

England won by 8 wickets

Appendix B

Australian Batting Averages in the Test Matches

	M	I	R	HS	NO	Average
D. G. Bradman	4	8	396	103*	1	56.57
S. J. McCabe	5	10	385	187*	1	42.77
L. S. Darling	2	4	148	85	0	37.00
W. M. Woodfull	5	10	305	73*	1	33.88
P. K. Lee	1	2	57	42	0	28.50
V. Y. Richardson	5	10	279	83	0	27.90
W. A. Oldfield	4	7	136	52	2	27.20
J. H. Fingleton	3	6	150	83	0	25.00
W. H. Ponsford	3	6	141	85	0	23.50
L. P. O'Brien	2	4	87	61	0	21.75
L. E. Nagel	1	2	21	21*	1	21.00
H. H. Alexander	1	2	17	17*	1	17.00
E. H. Bromley	1	2	33	26	0	16.50
A. F. Kippax	1	2	27	19	0	13.50
C. V. Grimmett	3	6	42	19	0	7.00
W. J. O'Reilly	5	10	61	19	0	6.10
T. W. Wall	4	8	42	20	1	6.00
H. S. Love	1	2	8	5	0	4.00
H. Ironmonger	4	8	13	8	3	2.60

* not out

Australian Bowling Averages in the Test Matches

	I	O	M	R	W	Average
T. W. Wall	7	160.1	33	409	16	25.56
W. J. O'Reilly	9	383.4	144	724	27	26.81
H. Ironmonger	8	245.1	96	405	15	27.00
P. K. Lee	2	52.4	14	163	4	40.75
D. G. Bradman	3	12	1	44	1	44.00
L. E. Nagel	1	43.4	9	110	2	55.00
C. V. Grimmett	5	147	41	326	5	65.20
S. J. McCabe	8	92.5	17	215	3	71.66
H. H. Alexander	2	46	2	154	1	154.00
A. G. Kippax	1	2	1	3	0	–
L. S. Darling	3	11	5	14	0	–
E. H. Bromley	1	10	4	19	0	–

England Batting Averages in the Tests against Australia

	M	I	R	HS	NO	Average
E. Paynter	3	5	184	83	2	61.33
W. R. Hammond	5	9	440	112	1	55.00
H. Sutcliffe	5	9	440	194	1	55.00
R. E. S. Wyatt	5	9	327	78	2	46.71
Nawab of Pataudi	2	3	122	102	0	40.66
M. Leyland	5	9	306	86	0	34.00
H. Verity	4	5	114	45	1	28.50
H. Larwood	5	7	145	98	1	24.16
G. O. Allen	5	7	163	48	0	23.28
D. R. Jardine	5	9	199	56	0	22.11
L. E. G. Ames	5	8	113	69	1	16.14
W. Voce	4	6	29	8	2	7.25

Also batted: W. E. Bowes 4* and 0*. T. B. Mitchell 0.

* not out

Appendix B

England Bowling Averages in the Tests against Australia

	I	O	M	R	W	Average
H. Larwood	10	220	42	644	33	19.51
T. B. Mitchell	2	21	5	60	3	20.00
H. Verity	8	135	54	271	11	24.63
W. Voce	8	133.3	23	407	15	27.13
G. O. Allen	10	170.6	29	593	21	28.23
W. R. Hammond	10	120.3	27	291	9	32.33
W. E. Bowes	2	23	2	70	1	70.00
R. E. S. Wyatt	1	2	0	12	0	–

True adventure – available in Panther Books

Henri Charrière

Papillon   £2.50 ☐
Banco   £1.95 ☐

Emmett Grogan

Ringolevio   £1.95 ☐

Alexander McKee

Into the Blue   £1.95 ☐

Eric Newby

The Last Grain Race   £1.95 ☐

Tristan Jones

A Steady Trade   £2.50 ☐
The Incredible Voyage   £2.50 ☐

Barrie Penrose

Stalin's Gold   £1.95 ☐

To order direct from the publisher just tick the titles you want
and fill in the order form.   **GF3781**

The best in biography from Panther Books

John Brooke
King George III   £1.95 ☐

J Bryan III and Charles J V Murphy
The Windsor Story   £2.95 ☐

Margaret Forster
The Rash Adventurer   £1.25 ☐

Antonia Fraser
Mary Queen of Scots   £3.95 ☐
Cromwell: Our Chief of Men   £3.95 ☐

Eric Linklater
The Prince in the Heather   £2.50 ☐

Henri Troyat
Catherine the Great   £2.95 ☐

Sir Arthur Bryant
Samuel Pepys: The Man in the Making   £3.95 ☐
Samuel Pepys: The Years of Peril   £3.95 ☐

To order direct from the publisher just tick the titles you want
and fill in the order form.   **GB181**

The best in biography from Panther Books

Lee McCann
Nostradamus: The Man Who Saw Through Time   £2.50   ☐

Larry Collins & Dominique Lapierre
Or I'll Dress You in Mourning   £1.25   ☐

Ladislas Farago
Patton: Ordeal and Triumph   £1.50   ☐

Hermann Hesse
A Pictorial Biography   £1.50   ☐

A E Hotchner
Papa Hemingway   £1.25   ☐

Nell Kimball
My Life as an American Madam   £1.50   ☐

Doris Lessing
In Pursuit of the English   £1.50   ☐

Stan Gébler Davies
James Joyce – A Portrait of the Artist   £1.95   ☐

Jean Stein & George Plimpton
Edie: An American Biography   £3.95   ☐

To order direct from the publisher just tick the titles you want
and fill in the order form.   **GB281**

All these books are available at your local bookshop or newsagent, or can be ordered direct from the publisher..

To order direct from the publisher just tick the titles you want and fill in the form below.

Name_____

Address _____

Send to:
Panther Cash Sales
PO Box 11, Falmouth, Cornwall TR10 9EN.

Please enclose remittance to the value of the cover price plus:

UK 45p for the first book, 20p for the second book plus 14p per copy for each additional book ordered to a maximum charge of £1.63.

BFPO and Eire 45p for the first book, 20p for the second book plus 14p per copy for the next 7 books, thereafter 8p per book.

Overseas 75p for the first book and 21p for each additional book.